The Language Experts

FRENCH2.0

The Interactive Language Course for the 21st Century

Berlitz Publishing

New York   London   Singapore

FRENCH 2.0

Contacting the Editors

Every effort has been made to provide accurate information in this publication, but changes are inevitable. The publisher cannot be responsible for any resulting loss, inconvenience or injury. We would appreciate it if readers would call our attention to any errors or outdated information by contacting Berlitz Publishing, e-mail: comments@berlitzpublishing.com

First Printing: January 2011
Printed in China

Publishing Director: Sheryl Olinsky Borg
Senior Editor/Project Manager: Lorraine Sova
Editorial: Andrea Pearman, Brian Jacobs, Rosi McNab, Christine Frohly
Cover and Interior Design: Leighanne Tillman
Interior Composition: Wee Design Group
Cover Photo: Chubbster.Shutterstock.2010
Production Manager: Elizabeth Gaynor

Contents

How to Use FRENCH2.0

FRENCH2.0 is an innovative, beginner-level course that features a multimedia approach to help you function in a wide variety of everyday situations with French speakers. You'll practice listening, speaking, reading and writing in French online and by following the book.

 Visit the 2.0 companion website, **www.berlitzhotspot.com**, for all online and downloadable content.

FRENCH2.0 is divided into 18 lessons. Each lesson focuses on an important theme, such as greetings and introductions, ordering food and shopping. The lessons include these features:

DIALOGUE

Real-life dialogues between native speakers

VOCABULARY

The lessons's key words and phrases

ACTIVITY

A fun way to practice your listening, speaking, reading and writing skills— in the book and online

DID YOU KNOW?

Cultural aspects of the major French-speaking countries

GRAMMAR

Quick and easy grammar explanations— in plain English

LEARNING TIP

Advice on how to remember your new language

PRONUNCIATION

A focus on the sounds of French

LEARN MORE

Practical ways to extend your language skills

 Check It!

A useful list of what you've accomplished in the lesson

BERLITZ HOTSPOT

Go to www.berlitzhotspot.com for...

 Social Networking
Prompts to start conversations
with your Hotspot friends

 Podcast
Downloadable info on French
culture and language

 Internet Activity
Explore real French websites

 Video
Animated scenes of culture and language in action

 Audio
For sections that are available with audio

You'll also find two tests in the book, after lessons 9 and 18. The tests
are an opportunity to confirm you've met the goals of the course. For your
reference, an answer key has been included, as well as up-to-date maps
of the major French-speaking countries.

FRENCH2.0 CD-ROM

In addition to online content, 2.0 includes a CD-ROM, at the back
of this book, with fun language-learning games, activities and
audio. Practice and reinforce the language you're learning!

Match It!
Play a French-language
memory game.

Quiz2.0
Test your knowledge
of French language,
grammar and culture.

Watch It!
Answer questions about
the French2.0 videos.

Listen Up!
Advance your listening
comprehension skills.

Speak Up!
Practice your French
pronunciation.

Pronunciation

This section is designed to make you familiar with the sounds of French using our simplified phonetic transcription. You'll find the pronunciation of the French letters and sounds explained below, together with their "imitated" equivalents.

In French, all syllables are pronounced the same, with no extra stress on any particular syllable. The French language contains nasal vowels, which are indicated in the pronunciation by a vowel symbol followed by an N. This N should not be pronounced strongly, but it is there to show the nasal quality of the previous vowel. A nasal vowel is pronounced simultaneously through the mouth and the nose.

In French, the final consonants of words are not always pronounced. When a word ending in a consonant is followed with a word beginning with a vowel, the two words are often run together. The consonant is therefore pronounced as if it begins the following word.

Example	Pronunciation
comment	koh-mawN
Comment allez-vous?	koh-mawN tah-lay-voo

CONSONANTS

Letter	Approximate Pronunciation	Symbol	Example	Pronunciation
cc	1. before e, i, like cc in accident	ks	accessible	ahk-seh-see-bluh
cc	2. elsewhere, like cc in accommodate	k	d'accord	dah-kohr
ch	1. like sh in shut	sh	chercher	shehr-shay
c	like s in sit	s	ça	sah
g	1. before e, i, y, like s in pleasure	zh	manger	mawN-zhay
g	2. before a, o, u, like g in go	g	garçon	gahr-sohN
h	always silent		homme	ohm
j	like s in pleasure	zh	jamais	zhah-may
qu	like k in kite	k	qui	kee
r	rolled in the back of the mouth, like gargling	r	rouge	roozh
w	usually like v in voice	v	wagon	vah-gohN

B, c, d, f, k, l, m, n, p, s, t, v, x and z are pronounced as in English.

4

VOWELS

Letter	Approximate Pronunciation	Symbol	Example	Pronunciation
a, à, â	between the a in hat and the a in father	ah	mari	mah-ree
e	sometimes like a in about	uh	je	zhuh
è, ê, e	like e in get	eh	même	mehm
é, ez	like a in late	ay	été	ay-tay
i	like ee in meet	ee	il	eel
o, ô	generally like o in roll	oh	donner	doh-nay
u	like ew in dew	ew	une	ewn

Sounds spelled with two or more letters

Letter	Approximate Pronunciation	Symbol	Example	Pronunciation
ai, ay, aient, ais, ait, aî, ei	1. like a in late	ay	j'ai vais	zhay vay
ai, ay, aient, ais, ait, aî, ei	2. like e in get	eh	chaîne peine	shehn pehn
(e)au	similar to o	oh	chaud	shoh
eu, eû œu	like u in fur but short like a puff of air	uh	euro	uh-roh
euil, euille	like uh + y	uhy	feuille	fuhy
ail, aille	like ie in tie	ie	taille	tie
ille	1. like yu in yucca	eeyuh	famille	fah-meeyuh
ille	2. like eel	eel	ville	veel
oi, oy	like w followed by the a in father	wah	moi	mwah
ou, où	like o in move or oo in hoot	oo	nouveau	noo-voh
ui	approximately like wee in between	wee	traduire	trah-dweer

Lesson 1 Hello!

Bonjour !

LESSON OBJECTIVES

Lesson 1 is about meeting people. When you have completed this lesson, you'll know how to:

- exchange greetings
- ask how someone is and tell him/her how you are
- say goodbye

DIALOGUE

 Listen to these people greeting each other.

Monsieur:	**Bonsoir, mademoiselle. Comment ça va ?** Good evening, miss. How are you?
Mademoiselle:	**Ça va bien, merci. Et vous ?** I'm fine, thank you. What about you?
Monsieur:	**Ça va.** I'm fine.

....

Monsieur:	**Bonjour, madame.** Hello, madam.
Madame:	**Bonjour, monsieur. Comment ça va ?** Hello, sir. How are you?
Monsieur:	**Ça va bien, merci.** I'm fine, thank you.

....

Monsieur:	**Au revoir, Céline. Bonne nuit.** Goodbye, Céline. Good night.
Madame:	**Bonne nuit !** Good night!

....

Monsieur:	**Salut, Nicole.** Hi, Nicole.
Madame:	**Salut, Alain.** Hi, Alain.
Monsieur:	**Ça va ?** How are you?
Madame:	**Ah oui, ça va bien, merci.** Yes, I'm fine, thank you.

1. DIALOGUE ACTIVITY

A. What time of day is it in each conversation?

B. In each conversation, are the people arriving or departing?

8

Use the following words and expressions to guide you through the lesson.

VOCABULARY

au revoir	goodbye	**mais**	but
la baguette	baguette	**merci**	thank you
bien	well	**Mesdames**	ladies
bonjour	good morning/ good day	**Messieurs (MM.)**	gentlemen
bonne nuit	good night (used late evening or when going to bed)	**Messieursdames**	ladies and gentlemen
		le monsieur	sir/man
		Monsieur (M.)	Mr./sir
bonsoir	good evening	**le nom**	name
le boulanger	baker	**non**	no
Ça va.	OK.	**oui**	yes
Ça va bien merci, et vous ?	Well, thank you, and you?	**pas mal**	not bad/OK
chez le boulanger	at the baker's	**salut**	hi/bye (used informally both as a greeting and farewell)
comme ci, comme ça	so so		
Comment ça va ?	How are you?	**s'il vous plaît**	please
un croissant	a croissant	**très**	very
deux	two	**très bien**	very well
et	and	**Voilà.**	Here you are.
la madame	madam/woman	**votre**	your
Madame (Mme)	Mrs./madam	**vous**	you (s., form./pl.)
Mademoiselle (Mlle)	miss/young lady		

Comment ça va ?

Ça va bien merci.

Abbreviations

f. feminine
form. formal
inf. informal
lit. literally
m. masculine
pl. plural
s. singular

DID YOU KNOW?

In France, it is polite to add *Monsieur, Madame,* etc., when greeting someone or saying goodbye.

2. LISTENING ACTIVITY

 Listen to these people coming into M. Albert's shop. What do they buy?
Match each dialogue to the correct image.

1

M. Albert:	**Bonjour, Mme Renoir. Ça va ?**
Mme Renoir:	**Pas mal, et vous, M. Albert ? Ça va ?**
M. Albert:	**Très bien, merci.**
Mme Renoir:	**Une baguette et six croissants.**
M. Albert:	**Une baguette et six croissants. Voilà !**
Mme Renoir:	**Au revoir, monsieur.**
M. Albert:	**Au revoir, madame.**

\

2

Mlle Meujot:	**Bonsoir, M. Albert.**
M. Albert:	**Ah, bonsoir, Mlle Meujot. Ça va ?**
Mlle Meujot:	**Oh oui pas mal. Et vous, monsieur ?**
M. Albert:	**Ça va très bien merci. Vous désirez ?**
Mlle Meujot:	**Deux baguettes.**
M. Albert:	**Deux baguettes ? Voilà.**
Mlle Meujot:	**Au revoir, monsieur.**

1 bag

3

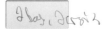

M. Albert:	**Bonsoir, messieursdames.**
Mme Duval:	**Bonsoir, M. Albert. Ça va ?**
M. Albert:	**Très bien, merci. Et vous ?**
Mme Duval:	**Oh oui, très bien. Deux baguettes, s'il vous plaît.**
M. Albert:	**C'est tout ?**
M. Duval:	**Et... et deux croissants.**
M. Albert:	**Voilà.**

3. LISTENING ACTIVITY

M. Albert is the baker. Listen to him greeting his customers and match each conversation with the appropriate image.

3 **Bonjour, monsieur. Vous désirez ?**

1 **Bonjour, mademoiselle. Vous voulez ?**

4 **Monsieur, madame, qu'est-ce que vous voulez ?**

2 **Bonjour, madame. Vous désirez ?**

5 **Messieursdames**

4. LISTENING ACTIVITY

Now listen to the conversations between M. Albert and his customers again and fill in the missing information according to the prompts.

M. Albert: **Bonjour, Mme Renoir. Ça va ?**

Mme Renoir: **Pas mal, et vous, M. Albert.** Ça va ? **?**
How are you?

M. Albert: **Très bien,** merci **.**
thank you

Mme Renoir: **Une** baguette **et six croissants.**
baguette

M. Albert: **Une baguette et** six croissants **. Voilà !**
six croissants

Mme Renoir: **Au revoir** monsieur **.**
sir

M. Albert: Au revoir **, madam.**
Goodbye

Mlle Meujot: Bonsoir **, M. Albert.**
Good evening

M. Albert: **Ah, bonsoir,** mademoiselle **Meujot. Ça va ?**
miss

11

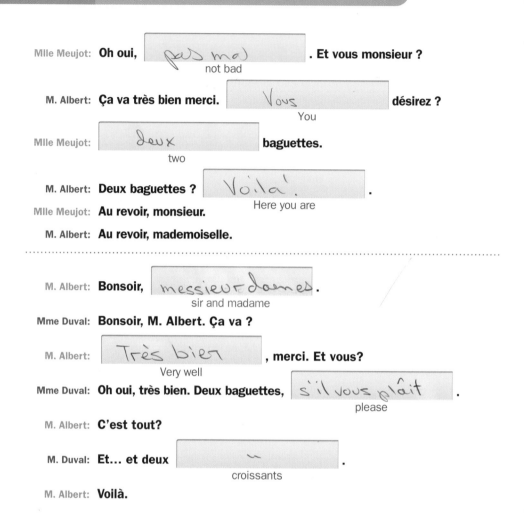

Mlle Meujot: **Oh oui,** _pas mal_ **. Et vous monsieur ?**
not bad

M. Albert: **Ça va très bien merci.** _Vous_ **désirez ?**
You

Mlle Meujot: _deux_ **baguettes.**
two

M. Albert: **Deux baguettes ?** _Voilà._
Here you are

Mlle Meujot: **Au revoir, monsieur.**

M. Albert: **Au revoir, mademoiselle.**

M. Albert: **Bonsoir,** _messieurdames_ .
sir and madame

Mme Duval: **Bonsoir, M. Albert. Ça va ?**

M. Albert: _Très bien_ **, merci. Et vous?**
Very well

Mme Duval: **Oh oui, très bien. Deux baguettes,** _s'il vous plaît_ .
please

M. Albert: **C'est tout?**

M. Duval: **Et... et deux** _____ .
croissants

M. Albert: **Voilà.**

5. READING ACTIVITY

Read the following conversations and put a (+) beside each speaker next to the line where he/she says if he/she is well, (✓) if he/she is OK, or (–) if the speaker is not so well.

Madame: **Bonjour, monsieur.**
Monsieur: **Bonjour, madame. Comment ça va ?**
Madame: **Ça va, merci. Et vous ?**   +
Monsieur: **Oui, ça va.**

Mlle Henry: **Bonsoir, M. Dupont.**
M. Dupont: **Ah, bonsoir Mlle Henry. Ça va ?**
Mlle Henry: **Oh oui, pas mal. Et vous, monsieur ?**   ✓
M. Dupont: **Ça va très bien, merci.**

M. Desart: **Bonsoir, madame.**

Mme Simon: **Bonsoir, M. Desart. Ça va ?**

M. Desart: **Très bien, merci. Et vous ?**   +

Mme Simon: **Oui, très, très bien.**

6. SPEAKING ACTIVITY

Et vous ? Comment ça va ? How would you answer this question?

7. WRITING ACTIVITY

Now it's your turn to ask these people how they are. Complete the conversations by filling in the missing words.

1

Vous: Monsieur   **Duval ! Bonjour ! Comment ça va ?**

Mme Duval: **Ça va. Et vous ?**

Vous: Ça va biens.   .

Mme Duval: **Au revoir,** [   ].
insert your name

Vous: **Au revoir,** Monsieu   **Duval.**

. . . .

2

Vous: Bonjour   **M. Meugeot.**

M. Meugeot: **Bonsoir,** [   ] **Ça va ?**
insert your name

Vous: Pas mad   **Et vous ? Ça va ?**

M. Meugeot: **Oui, merci. Au revoir,** [   ].
insert your name

Vous: Bonsoi   **M. Meugeot.**

. . . .

3

Vous: **Bonsoir** Madame **Renoir.**

M. Renoir: **Bonsoir,** _____. **Ça va ?**

insert your name

Vous: _____. **Je vais me coucher. Bonne nuit,**

_____ **Renoir !**

M. Renoir: **Bonne nuit.**

DID YOU KNOW?

The expression *Je vais me coucher* means, "I'm going to go to bed." (lit: I am going to put myself to bed.) The verb *se coucher* is called a reflexive verb. Reflexive verbs are used when the subject is performing the action on itself.

PRONUNCIATION

As French is not always pronounced as it is written, you need to spend a little extra time, especially at the beginning, practicing pronunciation and intonation.

Listen carefully and repeat the following words, trying to imitate the pronunciation:

monsieur	*madame*	*messieursdames*	*mesdemoiselles*
messieurs	*mesdames*	*mademoiselle*	

In French all syllables are stressed equally. Listen carefully and repeat these words, remembering to stress both parts of the word equally:

mon/sieur	*bon/jour*	*ba/guette*
ma/dame	*crois/sant*	

LEARNING TIP

Quite a few letters are not pronounced all the time in French. Listen to the dialogues carefully. You may find it helpful to write down how a word sounds to help you remember it. For example, you might think *monsieur* sounds like *mis-yeuh*.

Don't worry if you can't remember everything yet. You'll have many more opportunities to practice!

GRANMAR

In French all nouns are either masculine or feminine. The word for "a/one" before masculine nouns is *un*:

un croissant   a/one croissant

Before feminine nouns it is *une*:

une baguette   a/one baguette

To make the plural most French nouns add an *-s*:

deux baguettes   *deux croissants*

Note that the *s* is not pronounced.

8. SPEAKING ACTIVITY

Read the following phrases aloud, taking care to pronounce them as you heard in Activity 3.

Bonjour, Mme Renoir. Ça va?
Pas mal. Et vous, M. Albert? Ça va?
Très bien, merci.
Une baguette et six croissants.
Une baguette et six croissants. Voilà!
Au revoir monsieur.
Au revoir madame.

9. WRITING ACTIVITY

For each noun, write *un* if the noun is masculine and *une* if the noun is feminine, then write each noun in the plural.

article		plural noun
	baguette	
	boulanger	
	croissant	
	madame	
	monsieur	

Check It!

Test what you've learned in this lesson and review anything you're not sure of.

CAN YOU . . . ?

☐ **greet people**
Bonjour, madame.
Bonsoir, monsieur.
Bonne nuit, mademoiselle.
Salut !

☐ **ask someone how he/she is doing**
Ça va ?
Comment ça va ?

☐ **respond when someone asks how you are doing**
Oui, ça va.
Pas mal.
Très bien.

☐ **say thank you**
merci

☐ **say goodbye**
Au revoir, monsieur.
Salut !

BERLITZ HOTSPOT   Go to www.berlitzhotspot.com for...

 Social Networking
Share your thoughts on the French alphabet. Are any of the sounds confusing or challenging for you? Do you have any funny pronunciation stories? Share them with your new friends.

 Podcast 1
Bonjour !
Download this podcast.

 Internet Activity
Are you interested in learning more French last names? Go to **Berlitz Hotspot** for a list of sites with French names. Browse and pick three or four names you like. Practice greeting these people in the morning, afternoon and night and ask how they are.

 Video 1 – How to Kiss Hello
In France, friends, family members and close acquaintances normally greet each other with two kisses, one on each cheek, although people from some regions give three or four kisses. Watch the video to see how it's done.

Lesson 2 | I am...

Je suis...

LESSON OBJECTIVES

Lesson 2 is about people and places. When you have completed this lesson, you'll know how to:

- introduce yourself and others
- ask for and give information about countries and nationalities
- ask what languages someone speaks

DIALOGUE

 Listen to M. Martin asking these conference delegates to introduce themselves and say where they are from.

M. Martin: **Bienvenue à Paris. Voulez-vous vous présenter ? Vous êtes... ?**
Welcome to Paris. Can you please introduce yourselves? You are...?

M. Bernard: **Je suis Gilles Bernard et j'habite à Genève en Suisse. Je suis suisse.**
I am Gilles Bernard and I live in Geneva in Switzerland. I am Swiss.

M. Martin: **M. Bernard est suisse. Et vous êtes... ?**
M. Bernard is Swiss. And you are...?

Mlle Verlaine: **Je m'appelle Sylvie Verlaine et j'habite en France, à Paris.**
My name is Sylvie Verlaine and I live in France, in Paris.

M. Martin: **Mademoiselle Verlaine est française et elle habite à Paris. Et vous êtes madame... ?**
Mlle Verlaine is French and she lives in Paris. And you are Mrs...?

M. Bernard: **Je m'appelle Lucienne Briand. J'habite à Bruxelles en Belgique. Je suis belge.**
My name is Lucienne Briand. I live in Brussels in Belgium. I am Belgian.

M. Martin: **Et Mme Briand est belge. Et vous, monsieur ?**
And Mme Briand is Belgian. What about you, sir?

M. Millerioux: **J'habite à Québec, au Canada et je m'appelle Patrice Millerioux.**
I live in Quebec, in Canada and my name is Patrice Millerioux.

M. Martin: **M. Millerioux est canadien, d'origine française.**
M. Millerioux is Canadian of French origin.

1. DIALOGUE ACTIVITY

A. What are some of the cities that the delegates are from?

B. And the countries they are from?

Use the following words and expressions to guide you through the lesson.

VOCABULARY

à	at/in	en Belgique	in Belgium
au Brésil	in Brazil	en Espagne	in Spain
au Canada	in Canada	en France	in France
au Japon	in Japan	en Italie	in Italy
aux Antilles	in the West Indies	en Suisse	in Switzerland
aux États-Unis	in the United States	l'Espagne (f.)	Spain
l'Allemagne (f.)	Germany	espagnol/espagnole	Spanish
américain/américaine	American	les États-Unis	the United States
anglais/anglaise	English	être	to be
l'Angleterre (f.)	England	français/française	French
les Antilles (f., pl.)	the Antilles (West Indies)	la France	France
		l'Italie (f.)	Italy
belge	Belgian	italien/italienne	Italian
la Belgique	Belgium	le Japon	Japan
le Brésil	Brazil	japonais/japonaise	Japanese
brésilien/brésilienne	Brazilian	Je m'appelle...	My name is...
le Canada	Canada	Je suis...	I am...
canadien/canadienne	Canadian	J'habite...	I live...
comment	how	où	where
la conférence	conference/lecture	portugais/portugaise	Portuguese
en	in	suisse	Swiss
en Allemagne	in Germany	la Suisse	Switzerland
en Angleterre	in England	Voici...	Here is...

2. DIALOGUE ACTIVITY

 Listen to the conversation again and match each delegate with the flag representing his/her country. Then list the nationality for each.

A.

Gilles Bernard est

B.

Sylvie Verlaine est

C.

Lucienne Briand est

D.

Patrice Millerioux est

3. SPEAKING ACTIVITY 66 99

Prepare what you would say to introduce the four people above to a French colleague.

Example:

Je vous présente *M. Gilles Bernard.* Il est *suisse* et il habite à *Genève en Suisse.*

GRAMMAR

Sometimes the adjective changes for the feminine form. Make sure that you use the correct form of the adjective. For example, you would say: *M. Millerioux est canadien,* but if you were talking about his wife you would say: *Mme Millerioux est canadienne.*

4. SPEAKING ACTIVITY

 Sylvie Verlaine hasn't been paying attention and is asking you about the delegates. If she is right, say: *Oui, il est...* (if she is talking about a man) or *Oui, elle est...* (if she is talking about a woman). If she is wrong say *Non, il/elle n'est pas..., il/elle est....*

Example:

M. Bernard est américain ?   **Non, il n'est pas américain, il est suisse.**

Mme Briand est suisse ?

| |
| |

M. Millerioux est anglais ?

| |
| |

DID YOU KNOW?

 When talking about nationalities, a French speaker might describe himself or herself as a person of a particular country, *Je suis français/française* (I am French, m./f.), or say where he or she comes from, *Je viens de France* (I come from France). It is less common to use—as we do in English—the verb "to be" with a country of origin: *Je suis de France* (I am from France).

---

5. LISTENING ACTIVITY

Listen to these five contestants on a television quiz show. Where is each one from? What languages does each one speak? Complete the sentences.

A. Gerard: **Bonjour. Je m'appelle Gérard et je suis**

| |
. **J'habite à Rouen et je parle**

français et | | .

 Présentateur: **Ah, vous êtes français !**

B.

Anja: Moi ? Je [   ] Anja et

je [   ] Allemande.

J' [   ] à Berlin

[   ] Allemagne. Je parle

allemand et un peu [   ].

Présentateur: Vous êtes allemande ! Très bien. Et vous, monsieur ?

C.

Nigel: J' [   ] à New York

[   ] États-Unis.

Je m'appelle Nigel [   ] je suis

[   ].

Présentateur: Ah, vous êtes américain ! Et vous, vous êtes... ?

D.

Kenji: Je m'appelle Kenji et j'habite à Tokyo

[   ] Japon.

Je [   ] japonais et je parle

japonais et [   ].

Présentateur: Japonais...et vous, mademoiselle, vous êtes espagnole ?

E.

Rosa: Moi? Je m'appelle [   ].

Non, je ne suis pas espagnole. Je suis brésilienne.

J'habite à [   ] au

[   ]. Je parle portugais, anglais

et [   ] de français.

6. SPEAKING ACTIVITY

Now it's your turn. The presenter is asking you some questions. How would you answer?

Vous habitez à Londres ?

Parlez-vous français ?

Parlez-vous japonais ?

Comment vous appelez-vous ?

7. SPEAKING ACTIVITY

How would you ask each of these people his/her name, where he/she is from and the languages he/she speaks?

GRAMMAR

Words for nationalities and languages are not capitalized in French unless they are at the beginning of a sentence. For example, in English we write: "I am French. I speak French." In French, this is: *Je suis français. Je parle français.* The only other time you capitalize a nationality is when you use it as a noun. In English, we say "the Belgians." In French, *les Belges.*

Lesson 2   Je suis…

8. SPEAKING ACTIVITY

Now see if you can introduce yourself, give your name, say where you live and tell what nationality you are. Complete the sentences.

Je m'appelle…
J'habite à… en/au/aux…
Je suis…

PRONUNCIATION

Some pairs of words are pronounced as one, for example: *États-Unis, au revoir.* Listen carefully and repeat each phrase. Remember to stress all the syllables equally and to pronounce the words as one, where indicated.

Marc habite au Canada.
John habite aux États-Unis.
Lucy habite en Angleterre.
Lee habite au Japon.

The Definite Article   GRAMMAR

The word for "the" with masculine nouns is *le*:

le nom   the name   *le Canada*   Canada

and with feminine nouns it is *la*:

la France   France   *la Belgique*   Belgium

If the noun begins with a vowel or silent *h* (m. and f.) you use *l'*:

l'hôtel (m.)   the hotel   *l'Amérique (f.)*   America

The plural for both m. and f. is *les*:

les chambres (f.) the rooms   *les États-Unis (m.)* the United States

9. WRITING ACTIVITY

Insert *le, la* or *l'* (the) for each of the following countries.

	Allemagne
	Angleterre
	Antilles
	Belgique
	Brésil
	Canada
	Espagne
	États-Unis
	France
	Italie
	Japon
	Suisse

GRAMMAR

The word for "in":

- With feminine countries use *en*.

- With the names of towns and cities use *à*.

- With masculine and plural countries use the contraction *à* + the correct definite article:

à + le = au	*J'habite au Canada.*
à + les = aux	*J'habite aux États-Unis.*

10. WRITING ACTIVITY

Now write "in" each of the following countries, using *en, au, aux*. Check the grammar tip above if you need help.

	Allemagne		**Espagne**
	Angleterre		**États-Unis**
	Antilles		**France**
	Belgique		**Italie**
	Brésil		**Japon**
	Canada		**Suisse**

Nationalities & Languages

GRAMMAR

Saying what nationality you are:

If you are a man:	*Je suis américain/français.* I am American/French.
If you are a woman:	*Je suis américaine/française.* I am American/French.

GRAMMAR

The names of the languages are the same as the masculine form of the nationality:

Je parle français.   *Je parle anglais.*

Pronouns

Singular   Plural

je	I		*nous*	we
tu	you (sing. inf.)		*vous*	you (pl. or sing. form.)
il	he		*ils*	they (m.)
elle	she		*elles*	they (f.)

Elles is used only when talking about two or more females. If the company is mixed, use *ils*.

The Verb to Be

être   to be

je suis	I am		*nous sommes*	we are
tu es	you are		*vous êtes*	you are
il est	he is		*ils sont*	they (m.) are
elle est	she is		*elles sont*	they (f.) are

Negation

To make a negative in French you add *ne* (or *n'* before a vowel) in front of the verb and *pas* after the verb:

Vous êtes suisse?	*Non, je ne suis pas suisse.*
Il est japonais?	*Non, il n'est pas japonais.*

Plural Adjectives

Remember that adjectives must agree with both the gender and number of the nouns they describe. To form a plural adjective, add –*s* to the end of the masculine/feminine singular adjective, unless the adjective already ends in –*s*, in which case you don't need to change anything. For example:

Elle est américaine.	*Elles sont américaines.*
Il est canadien.	*Ils sont canadiens.*

11. WRITING ACTIVITY

For each of the following people, fill in the correct information using the prompts. The first one has been done for you.

Japanese:

Je suis japonaise .

Je parle .

Italian:

Je suis .

Je parle .

Belgian (French):

Je suis .

Je parle .

German:

Je suis .

Je parle .

Brazilian

Je suis .

Je parle .

Swiss (French):

Je suis .

Je parle .

Canadian (English):

Je suis .

Je parle .

12. SPEAKING ACTIVITY

Translate the following sentences, using the correct pronouns and conjugation of *être* given the prompts.

Example:

We are Katja, Anja and Christian. We are not German. We are Swiss.

Nous sommes Katja, Anja et Christian. Nous ne sommes pas allemands. Nous sommes suisses.

1. They are Claudia and Paula. They are Spanish.

   You are Giuseppe. You are Italian.

3. He is Timiko. Is he Japanese?

   She is Gisele. Is she Brazilian?

5. I am Alexis. I am Belgian. I am not French.

Check It!

Test what you've learned in this lesson and review anything you're not sure of.

CAN YOU . . . ?

☐ **introduce yourself and others**
Je suis...
Je m'appelle...
Je vous présente M. Gilles Bernard.

☐ **ask for and give information about countries and nationalities**
Je viens de France. Je suis français/française.
J'habite au Canada, mais je suis japonais/japonaise.
Il est allemand.

☐ **ask what languages someone speaks and say what languages you speak**
Vous parlez français ?
Je parle anglais et un peu de français.

☐ **say "in" a country**
Je suis en France.
Aux États-Unis...

☐ **name the pronouns**
je, tu, il/elle, nous, vous, ils/elles

☐ **conjugate the verb *être***
je suis, tu es, il/elle est, nous sommes, vous êtes, ils/elles sont

☐ **say sentences in the negative**
Non, je ne suis pas suisse.
Non, il n'est pas japonais.

 BERLITZ HOTSPOT   Go to www.berlitzhotspot.com for...

 Social Networking
Go to **Berlitz Hotspot** and introduce yourself. Use this model: *Salut, je m'appelle* (your name). *Je viens de* (your location). If you prefer to be a bit more formal, use *Bonjour* instead of *Salut*.

 Internet Activity
Would you like to learn more country names and nationalities?
Go to **Berlitz Hotspot** for a list of sites with maps in French.
Practice making questions or statements regarding the countries and their residents, like *Vous êtes canadien ?* or *Elle habite aux États-Unis. Elle est américaine ?*

Podcast 2
French Around the World
Download the podcast.

Lesson 3 — At the Hotel

À l'hôtel

LESSON OBJECTIVES

Lesson 3 is about communicating with people. When you have completed this lesson, you'll know how to:

- talk on the telephone
- spell
- count to 20

DIALOGUE

 Listen to this group of tourists at the reception desk of your hotel.

Concierge: **Mme Graham, comment ça s'écrit ?**
How do you spell Mme Graham?

Mme Graham: **Graham, G-R-A-H-A-M**

Concierge: **Pouvez-vous épeler ça, monsieur ?**
Can you spell that, sir?

Mme Graham: **Schwartz, S-C-H-W-A-R-T-Z**

Concierge: **Merci, et madame ?**
Thank you, and madam?

Mme Fernandez: **Fernandez, F-E-R-N-A-N-D-E-Z**

Concierge: **Et le monsieur ?**
What about the gentleman?

M. Rossellini: **Rossellini, R-O-S-S-E-L-L-I-N-I**

Concierge: **R, O, deux S, E, deux L, I, N, I**
R, O, two S's, E two L's, I, N, I

M. Rossellini: **C'est exact.**
That's right.

Concierge: **Et le monsieur écossais ?**
What about the Scottish gentleman?

M. Macintosh: **Macintosh, M-A-C-I-N-T-O-S-H**

Concierge: **Bon. Merci, monsieur.**
Good. Thank you, sir.

M. Macintosh: **Je vous en prie.**
You are welcome.

1. DIALOGUE ACTIVITY

A. **What are the names of the guests?**

B. **How do you ask someone to spell out a word?**

Use the following words and expressions to guide you through the lesson.

la chambre	room/bedroom	**la salle de bains**	bathroom
la douche	shower	**la société**	company/business
l'hôtel (m.)	hotel	**s'il vous plaît**	please
le numéro	number	**ou**	or
la réception	reception	**venir**	to come
la réservation	reservation		

2. LISTENING ACTIVITY

Listen to the alphabet and pick out the letters you need to spell your own name. Write down the sound of the letters you find difficult, for example *e* sounds like *euh* and *i* sounds like *ee*.

3. SPEAKING ACTIVITY

The clerk from the hotel is having trouble understanding some of the names and asks you to spell them. Spell them aloud.

4. SPEAKING ACTIVITY

Now you check in. Listen to the clerk's questions and answer them. Use the following phrases if you don't understand or if she is talking too fast.

Concierge: **Vous avez une reservation ?**
Do you have a reservation?

Vous: Answer her.

Concierge: **Votre nom, s'il vous plaît.**
Your name, please.

Vous: Tell her your name.

Concierge: **Comment ça s'écrit ?**
How do you spell it?

Vous: Tell her how you spell it.

Concierge: **Vous venez d'où ?**
Where are you from?

Vous: **Parlez plus lentement s'il vous plaît.**
Speak more slowly, please.

Concierge: **Vous venez d'où ?**
Where are you from?

Vous: Tell her what nationality you are.

Concierge: **Vous habitez où ?**
Where do you live?

Vous: Tell her where you live.

Concierge: **Vous voulez une chambre avec douche ou salle de bains ?**
Do you want a room with a shower or a bathroom?

Vous: Answer her.

Concierge: **Chambre numéro quinze.**
Room number 15.

Numbers 1–20

1	un	6	six	11	onze	16	seize
2	deux	7	sept	12	douze	17	dix-sept
3	trois	8	huit	13	treize	18	dix-huit
4	quatre	9	neuf	14	quatorze	19	dix-neuf
5	cinq	10	dix	15	quinze	20	vingt

5. LISTENING ACTIVITY

The clerk is telling guests their room numbers. Listen and write them down.

A. **Fernandez est à la chambre numéro** _____ .

B. **Macintosh est à la chambre numéro** _____ .

C. **Schwartz est à la chambre numéro** _____ .

D. **Rossellini est à la chambre numéro** _____ .

E. **Graham est à la chambre numéro** _____ .

6. SPEAKING ACTIVITY

The tour guide needs to distribute the program for the visit. Tell him which rooms each person is in. Read the names and numbers aloud.

7. SPEAKING ACTIVITY

Listen to Martin Smith on the telephone, asking to speak to M. Duval at the Sociéte Beauvin.

Madame:	**Allô, Société Beauvin.**
Martin Smith:	**Je peux parler avec monsieur Duval ?**
Madame:	**C'est de la part de qui ?**
Martin Smith:	**Je m'appelle Martin Smith.**
Madame:	**Vous pouvez l'épeler ?**
Martin Smith:	**Martin, M-A-R-T-I-N, Smith, S-M-I-T-H**
Madame:	**Ne quittez pas.**

Now imagine you are calling M. Duval.

Madame:	**Allô, Société Beauvin.**
Vous:	Ask if you can speak to monsieur Duval.
Madame:	**C'est de la part de qui ?**
Vous:	Say your name.
Madame:	**Vous pouvez l'épeler ?**
Vous:	Spell it.
Madame:	**Ne quittez pas.**

LEARNING TIP

Try to spend a few minutes each day listening to the dialogues so that you become more familiar with the sound of French. You may find it difficult at first to distinguish individual words, but don't be discouraged. Keep listening and you will soon be able to recognize what is being said, which is the first step in learning a new language.

French Vowels

PRONUNCIATION

Accents are used with some letters in French to modify their sound. The accents are called:

accent aigu	é
accent grave	à è ù
cédille	ç
accent circonflexe	â ê î ô û

é   is pronounced *ay*, as in *écrit, activité*.

è   is pronounced *eh*, as in *frère*, brother, *Frère Jacques*.

ç   is pronounced like *s* in "so": *Ça va, français, garçon*.

The accent *circonflexe* does not change the sound.

The letters *s* and *t* at the end of a word are not usually pronounced: *vou(s), nui(t), françai(s)*.

When *s* is followed by *e* it is pronounced: *Il est français*. (*S* is not sounded.) *Elle est française*. (*S* is sounded.)

Listen carefully and repeat these phrases:

Il est français. Elle est française.
Il est anglais. Elle est anglaise.
Il est japonais. Elle est japonaise.

GRAMMAR

Remember: the word for "the" with masculine nouns is *le* and with feminine nouns is *la: le nom, la chambre*.

If the word begins with a vowel or silent *h* (m. and f.) use *l'*: *l'hôtel, l'Amérique*.

The plural for both m. and f. nouns is *les: les noms, les chambres*.

	m.	f.	pl.
a/one	*un*	*une*	*des* (some)
the	*le (l')*	*la (l')*	*les*

Check It!

Test what you've learned in this lesson and review anything you're not sure of.

CAN YOU . . . ?

☐ **use phone-related vocabulary**
Allô ?
Je peux parler avec M. Duval ?
C'est de la part de qui ?
Vous pouvez l'épeler ?
Ne quittez pas !

☐ **say the French alphabet**
A, B, C...

☐ **ask someone how to spell his/her name**
Comment ça s'écrit ?
Pouvez-vous épeler ça ?

☐ **understand hotel-related vocabulary**
Vous avez une reservation ?
Votre nom, s'il vous plaît ?
Vous voulez une chambre avec douche
   ou salle de bains ?

☐ **answer questions about yourself**
Vous venez d'où ?
Vous habitez où ?

☐ **understand numbers to 20**
Chambre numéro quinze.

☐ **let someone know that you do not understand what he/she is saying**
Je ne comprends pas.
Parlez plus lentement, s'il vous plaît.

Learn More +

Search the internet for French language newspapers and go to the foreign news section, usually called *International*. Scan the headlines and articles and see how many country names you recognize.

BERLITZ HOTSPOT   Go to www.berlitzhotspot.com for...

Social Networking
Go to **Berlitz Hotspot** and share your thoughts on the French alphabet. Are any of the sounds confusing or challenging for you? Do you have any funny pronunciation stories? Share them with your Hotspot friends.

Podcast 3
Allô ? Download the podcast.

Internet Activity
How about some more practice? Return to the links to the French name sites at **Berlitz Hotspot.** Pick ten names and spell them aloud. Then practice having a telephone conversation using some of the names you like.

Video 2 – Finger Counting
People the world over use their fingers to count, but not always in the same direction. The French start counting with their thumb.

Lesson 4 At the Café

Au café

LESSON OBJECTIVES

Lesson 4 is about ordering in a café. When you have completed this lesson, you'll know how to:

- order breakfast or a snack in a café
- count to 60
- ask for prices

DIALOGUE

M. and Mme Albert are at a café in Rouen with their daughters Nathalie and Delphine. Listen to them ordering.

M. Albert:	**Monsieur ?**
	Sir?
Serveur:	**Messieursdames. Vous désirez ?**
	Ladies and gentlemen, what would you like?
M. Albert:	**Je voudrais un café.**
	I would like a coffee.
Mme Albert:	**Un crème pour moi.**
	A coffee with milk for me.
Serveur:	**Bon, un crème. Grand ou petit ?**
	OK, a coffee with milk. Large or small?
Mme Albert:	**Grand….et….un jus d'orange pour Nathalie.**
	Large…and…an orange juice for Nathalie.
Serveur:	**Un café, un grand crème et un jus d'orange.**
	A coffee, a large coffee with milk, and an orange juice.
Mme Albert:	**Et pour toi Delphine ?**
	And for you Delphine?
Delphine:	**Je voudrais un chocolat chaud.**
	I would like a hot chocolate.
Serveur:	**Un chocolat chaud. C'est tout ?**
	One hot chocolate. Is that all?
M. Albert:	**Avez-vous des croissants ?**
	Do you have croissants?
Serveur:	**Oui, bien sûr.**
	Yes, of course.
M. Albert:	**Quatre croissants, s'il vous plaît.**
	Four croissants please.
Serveur:	**Quatre croissants…tout de suite.**
	Four croissants…right away.

Use the following words and expressions to guide you through the lesson.

VOCABULARY

l'addition (f.)	bill	plate	still/noncarbonated
la bière	beer	l'express (m.)	espresso
le café	coffee	grand	big
le chocolat chaud	hot chocolate	le jus d'orange	orange juice
le coca	cola	du lait	some milk
le crème	coffee with milk	l'orange pressée (f.)	freshly squeezed orange
le croissant	croissant	petit	small
le déca	decaffeinated coffee	le thé	tea
de l'eau (minérale)	some (mineral) water	le thé au lait	tea with milk
gazeuse	sparkling/carbonated		

1. DIALOGUE ACTIVITY

A. What does each person order to drink at the café?

B. Do they order anything to eat?

DID YOU KNOW?

Un café is a small black coffee, *un express* is an espresso and *un crème* is a coffee with a lot of milk or cream. You will often be offered a choice of a large or small *crème: Grand ou petit ?* If you want a larger American-style coffee, ask for a *café allongé,* which is an espresso served with hot water.

2. LISTENING ACTIVITY

 Now you are going to hear some of the other people in the café. What do they order?

1.

Serveur:	**Vous désirez, monsieur ?**
Monsieur:	**Deux crèmes.**
Serveur:	**Grands ou petits ?**
Monsieur:	**Grands.**

2.

Madame:	**Monsieur, un café, un chocolat et deux croissants.**
Serveur:	**Un café, un chocolat et deux croissants. C'est tout ?**
Madame:	**Oui, c'est tout.**

3.

Serveur:	**Vous désirez ?**
Madame:	**Une bière et de l'eau minérale.**
Serveur:	**Gazeuse ou non gazeuse ?**
Madame:	**Gazeuse.**
Serveur:	**Une bière et de l'eau minérale gazeuse. Très bien.**

4.

Serveur:	**Madame ?**
Madame:	**Un jus d'orange.**
Serveur:	**C'est tout ?**
Madame:	**Non, un croissant.**
Serveur:	**Un jus d'orange et un croissant.**

5.

Monsieur:	**Un déca, un grand crème et un thé au lait.**
Serveur:	**Un déca et un grand crème...et un thé au lait. C'est tout ?**
Monsieur:	**Avez-vous des croissants ?**
Serveur:	**Oui, bien sûr.**
Monsieur:	**Deux croissants alors.**
Serveur:	**Un déca, un grand crème, un thé au lait et deux croissants.**

6.

Serveur: **Messieursdames ?**

Madame: **Quatre cafés et quatre croissants.**

Serveur: **Ah ! Je regrette, je n'ai plus de croissants.**

Madame: **Bon, quatre cafés alors.**

3. SPEAKING ACTIVITY

You are in a café in France with some friends, who want you to order for them. Write down a list of what they want and practice what you would say to the waiter, then check the audio to see if you got it right. Repeat the phrases and imitate the speaker as much as possible to practice your pronunciation and intonation skills.

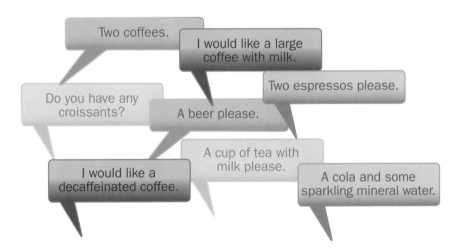

Two coffees.

I would like a large coffee with milk.

Two espressos please.

Do you have any croissants?

A beer please.

A cup of tea with milk please.

I would like a decaffeinated coffee.

A cola and some sparkling mineral water.

4. SPEAKING ACTIVITY

Listen and learn the numbers 20 through 60. Practice saying each number aloud after you hear it.

20	vingt	24	vingt-quatre	28	vingt-huit	50	cinquante
21	vingt et un	25	vingt-cinq	29	vingt-neuf	60	soixante
22	vingt-deux	26	vingt-six	30	trente		
23	vingt-trois	27	vingt-sept	40	quarante		

5. SPEAKING ACTIVITY

 These are the winning numbers in the lottery this week. First think of how you would pronounce them in French, and say them out loud. Then listen to the audio file to correct your pronunciation.

Vingt-quatre (24)
Trente-six (36)
Vingt-huit (28)
Quarante-sept (47)
Trente-neuf (39)
Vingt et un (21)

DID YOU KNOW?

In France, the currency symbol is written after the price, and the decimal point is replaced by a comma. So, you'll see, for example, *1,50€*, which is pronounced *un euro cinquante*.

6. SPEAKING ACTIVITY

 Now it's time for M. Albert to pay. Listen as he asks for the bill, then answer the questions.

M. Albert: **L'addition, s'il vous plaît.**

Serveur: **Un café, un grand crème, un jus d'orange, et quatre croissants, ça fait neuf euros vingt.**

M. Albert: **Tenez, dix euros.**

Serveur: **Merci monsieur. Au revoir et bonne journée.**

What drinks were ordered at the café?

How much does M. Albert have to pay?

PRONUNCIATION

 Listen carefully to distinguish between the pronunciation of *un* and *une*. Write down what they sound like if you find that helpful. Now practice saying these words:

> un thé   une bière
> un café   une orange

Remember how some groups of words are pronounced as one. Listen and repeat these phrases:

> *C'est tout ?*
> *Tout de suite.*
> *S'il vous plaît.*

GRAMMAR

To make the plural, you usually add *s* to the end of the word, as in English:

un crème   *deux crèmes*
un café   *deux cafés*

But the *s* ending is not pronounced.

All nouns in French are either masculine or feminine.

The definite article "the" and indefinite article "a" have different forms in French depending on whether the noun is masculine or feminine:

With masculine words:		With feminine words:	
un café	a coffee	*une bière*	a beer
le café	the coffee	*la bière*	the beer

Use *l'* before words that begin with a vowel or silent *h* (masculine or feminine):

| *un hôtel* | a hotel | *l'hôtel* | the hotel |

DID YOU KNOW?

 Many travelers are unaware that gratuity (and tax) is included in the price of food at restaurants in France. It is customary, however, to leave some change, up to one or two euros, if you are happy with the service. This "tip" is called *un pourboire*.

Check It!

Test what you've learned in this lesson and review anything you're not sure of.

CAN YOU . . . ?

☐ **ask what someone wants**
Vous désirez ?

☐ **ask for something to eat and drink**
Mademoiselle, une bière et de l'eau minérale, s'il vous plaît.
Un déca, un grand crème et un thé au lait.

☐ **ask if that's all**
C'est tout ?

☐ **say that you don't want (to order) anything else**
Oui, c'est tout.

☐ **say that you want one/some of something**
Je voudrais un croissant.
Deux crèmes, s'il vous plaît.

☐ **say the numbers up to 60**
vingt-huit (28)
quarante-sept (47)

☐ **understand prices**
Ça fait neuf euros vingt.

BERLITZ HOTSPOT   Go to www.berlitzhotspot.com for...

Social Networking
Tell your Hotspot friends about what foods or drinks you like to order in a café.

Podcast 4
Un café, s'il vous plaît.
Download the podcast.

Internet Activity
Are you interested in café culture? Go to **Berlitz Hotspot** for links to some French cafés. Have a look at the sites and practice ordering some of the items that you know using *Je voudrais...* and don't forget to ask for the bill, *L'addition, s'il vous plaît.*, before leaving.

Video 3 – Getting the Waiter's Attention
In France, the waiter/waitress will only stop by your table to take your order and serve you, and to provide the bill. If you need help while dining, you need to get the waiter's attention by signaling with your hand. Watch the video to see how it's done.

Lesson 5 At the Brasserie

À la brasserie

DIALOGUE

Listen to these two customers in the brasserie asking what kinds of sandwiches are available. Notice that the customers speak to each other using the informal you because they are friends.

Madame:	**Monsieur s'il vous plaît.** Excuse me sir.
Serveur:	**Bonjour, messieursdames.** **Vous désirez ?** Good day ladies and gentlemen. What would you like?
Madame:	**Vous avez des sandwichs ?** Do you have sandwiches?
Serveur:	**Oui, bien sûr.** Yes, of course.
Madame:	**Qu'est-ce que vous avez comme** **sandwichs ?** What kind of sandwiches do you have?
Serveur:	**Jambon, fromage, saucisson.** Ham, cheese, sausage.
Madame:	**Un sandwich au jambon pour moi.** **Et pour toi ?** A ham sandwich for me. And for you?
Monsieur:	**Un sandwich au fromage pour moi.** A cheese sandwich for me.
Serveur:	**Un sandwich au jambon et un sandwich au fromage.** **Et comme boisson ?** One ham sandwich and one cheese sandwich. And to drink?
Monsieur:	**Une pression pour moi...et pour toi ?** A draft beer for me...and for you?
Madame:	**Un verre de vin rouge.** A glass of red wine.

DID YOU KNOW?

Brasseries were originally places where you could buy beer, but now they have become popular eating places where you can get a quick meal without paying restaurant prices.

Use the following words and expressions to guide you through the lesson.

VOCABULARY

l'ami/l'amie	friend	l'omelette (f.)	omelet
aussi	also	au jambon	with ham
avec	with	aux fines herbes	with mixed herbs
la bière pression	draft beer	nature	plain
la boisson	drink	le pichet (de vin)	pitcher (of wine)
la bouteille (de vin rouge/blanc)	bottle (of red/white wine)	la portion de frites	portion of fries
		rien	nothing
la crème Chantilly	vanilla-flavored sweetened whipped cream	la salade	salad
		aux trois fromages	with three cheeses
le dessert	dessert	de fruits de mer	seafood
le fromage	cheese	niçoise	with tuna and olives
la glace	ice cream		
à la banane	banana flavored	le sandwich	sandwich
au chocolat	chocolate flavored	le saucisson	sausage/salami
à la fraise	strawberry flavored	le steak frites	steak and fries
aux pistaches	pistachio flavored	la tarte aux pommes	apple pie
à la vanille	vanilla flavored	le thé au citron	tea with lemon
le hamburger	hamburger	le verre (de vin)	glass (of wine)
le milk-shake	milkshake	le vin (rouge/blanc)	(red/white) wine

1. DIALOGUE ACTIVITY

What do the customers order to drink?

And to eat?

49

2. LISTENING ACTIVITY

Listen to the dialogue again and fill in the blanks. Then listen to the conversation again to check your answers.

Madame: **Monsieur** [_____].

Serveur: **Bonjour, messieursdames. Vous désirez ?**

Madame: **Vous avez des** [_____] **?**

Serveur: **Oui, bien sûr.**

Madame: [_____] **comme sandwichs ?**

Serveur: **Jambon, fromage, saucisson.**

Madame: **Un sandwich au** [_____] **pour moi. Et pour toi ?**

Monsieur: **Un sandwich au** [_____] **pour moi.**

Serveur: **Un sandwich au jambon et un sandwich au fromage.**

Et comme [_____] **?**

Monsieur: **Une pression pour moi...et pour toi ?**

Madame: **Un verre de** [_____] **rouge.**

3. SPEAKING ACTIVITY

What would you say to find out what's available at the *Brasserie Dupont*? How would you ask about the following items?

1. [_____]   4. [_____]

2. [_____]   5. [_____]

3. [_____]

4. WRITING ACTIVITY

Now choose something for yourself and a friend. Write down what you would order, then practice aloud what you would say.

Serveur: **Messieursdames, vous désirez ?**

Vous: **Je voudrais** [   ] **pour moi et**

[   ] **pour mon ami/amie.**

5. LISTENING ACTIVITY

Listen to the other people in the brasserie giving their orders and write down what they would like.

1. [   ]

Serveur: **Vous désirez, monsieur ?**
Monsieur: **Qu'est-ce que vous avez comme salades ?**
Serveur: **Salade niçoise, salade aux fruits de mer, salade aux trois fromages.**
Monsieur: **Une salade niçoise.**
Serveur: **Et comme boisson ?**
Monsieur: **De l'eau minérale.**
Serveur: **Gazeuse ?**
Monsieur: **Oui.**

2. [   ]

Serveur: **Vous désirez ?**
Madame: **Ben...je voudrais un steak frites.**
Serveur: **Et avec ça ?**
Madame: **Hum...Un pichet de vin rouge.**

3. [   ]

Serveur: **Vous désirez, messieursdames ?**
Monsieur #1: **Un hamburger pour moi et...**
Monsieur #2: **Pour moi un hamburger aussi...et une portion de frites.**

Serveur:	Grande ou petite ?
Monsieur #2:	Grande.
Serveur:	Et comme boisson ?
Monsieur #1:	Un coca.
Monsieur #2:	Qu'est-ce que vous avez comme milk-shakes ?
Serveur:	Fraise, vanille, banane, chocolat.
Monsieur #2:	Un milk shake à la vanille.

4.

Serveur:	Vous désirez, mesdames ?
Madame #1:	Je voudrais une omelette. Qu'est-ce que vous avez comme omelettes ?
Serveur:	Omelette nature, omelette au jambon, omelette au fromage, omelette aux fines herbes.
Madame #1:	Une omelette aux fines herbes.
Madame #2:	Et pour moi, une salade aux fruits de mer.
Serveur:	Et comme boisson ?
Madame #1:	Un thé au citron.
Madame #2:	Une bière.
Serveur:	En bouteille ou pression ?
Madame #2:	Une pression.

6. LISTENING ACTIVITY

 What desserts do they choose?

1.

Serveur:	Et comme dessert, monsieur ?
Monsieur:	Qu'est-ce que vous avez comme glaces ?
Serveur:	Glaces à la vanille, au chocolat, à la fraise, aux pistaches.
Monsieur:	Une glace à la fraise.

2.

| Serveur: | Voulez-vous un dessert, madame ? |
| Madame: | Merci. |

3.

Serveur:	**Voulez-vous un dessert Messieurs ?**
Monsieur #1:	**Qu'est-ce que vous avez comme desserts ?**
Serveur:	**Des glaces, une tarte au citron, une tarte aux pommes.**
Monsieur #1:	**La tarte aux pommes.**
Monsieur #2:	**Moi aussi, la tarte aux pommes.**

4.

Serveur:	**Vous voulez un dessert?**
Madame #1:	**Tarte au citron pour moi.**
Madame #2:	**Et je voudrais une glace au chocolat.**

Which would you choose for yourself and a friend?

Serveur:	**Vous voulez un dessert?**
Vous:	

DID YOU KNOW?

Merci means "No thank you" when you have been offered something. If you want what you have been offered say: *S'il vous plaît.*

7. SPEAKING ACTIVITY

Listen to the numbers 60 through 100. Practice saying them out loud.

60	soixante	75	soixante-quinze	81	quatre-vingt-un
70	soixante-dix	76	soixante-seize	90	quatre-vingt-dix
71	soixante et onze	77	soixante-dix-sept	91	quatre-vingt-onze
72	soixante-douze	78	soixante-dix-huit	99	quatre-vingt-dix-neuf
73	soixante-treize	79	soixante-dix-neuf	100	cent
74	soixante-quatorze	80	quatre-vingts		

8. SPEAKING ACTIVITY

For each of the bottles of wine answer the question: *Ça coûte combien ?* (How much does it cost?) Spell out the numbers of each price and practice saying them aloud, e.g., *Le vin rouge coûte...* (The red wine costs...)

9. READING ACTIVITY

Which is the right bill for each table?

Table une

Serveur: **Un sandwich au jambon et un sandwich au fromage, une pression et un verre de vin rouge. Ça fait quatorze euros quarante.**

Table deux

Serveur: **Une salade niçoise et de l'eau minérale gazeuse. Ça fait neuf euros.**

Table trois

Serveur: **Un steak frites et un pichet de vin rouge. Ça fait seize euros cinquante.**

Table quatre

Serveur: **Deux hamburgers, une grande portion de frites, un coca et un milk-shake à la vanille. Ça fait douze euros soixante.**

Table cinq

Serveur: **Une omelette aux fines herbes, une salade aux fruits de mer, un thé au citron et une pression. Ça fait dix-sept euros soixante-dix.**

PRONUNCIATION

More practice with *un* and *une*. Remember *un* is used with masculine words and *une* is used with feminine words.

Listen to these phrases and practice saying them aloud:

> *un verre de vin rouge*
> *un café*
> *un sandwich au jambon*
> *une tarte aux pommes*
> *une glace au chocolat*
> *une omelette aux fines herbes*

GRAMMAR

The word for "the" with masculine words is *le* and with feminine words it is *la*. The word for "a" with masculine words is *un* and with feminine words it is *une*. The plural forms for both masculine and feminine words are *les* (the) and *des* (some).

	m.	f.	pl.
the	*le sandwich*	*la glace*	*les sandwichs, les glaces*
a/some	*un sandwich*	*une glace*	*des sandwichs, des glaces*

When talking about flavors and fillings, you use *à* + *le/la/les*:

une glace à la vanille   a vanilla ice cream

Now see what happens to *à* in front of *le* and *les*:

	m.	f.	pl.
	à + le = au	*à la*	*à + les = aux*
	le chocolat	*la vanille*	*les pistaches*
une glace	*au chocolat*	*à la vanille*	*aux pistaches*

LEARNING TIP

To remember numbers in French, say them in French when using these words in your daily life.

Check It!

Test what you've learned in this lesson and review anything you're not sure of.

CAN YOU . . . ?

☐ **ask what is available**
Qu'est-ce que vous avez comme… ?
Et comme boisson ?

☐ **accept an offer**
S'il vous plaît.

☐ **reject an offer**
Merci.

☐ **count to 100**
Ça fait vingt-trois euros soixante.
Ça coûte soixante-dix euros.

 BERLITZ HOTSPOT   Go to www.berlitzhotspot.com for...

 Social Networking
Chat with your Hotspot friends about the different kinds of French food you've sampled or would like to try. Ask them about their French food and drink preferences.

Podcast 5
Red, White or Bubbly?
Download this podcast.

 Internet Activity
Do you like French food? Go to **Berlitz Hotspot** for links to some famous French restaurants. Have a look at the sites and practice ordering some dishes that sound interesting to you.

Chez le marchand de journaux

Lesson 6 is about making small purchases. When you have completed this lesson, you'll know how to:

- ask for items you want to buy at a shop
- ask for prices

DIALOGUE

 Listen to Mme Millerioux make a purchase at the newsstand.

La marchande de journaux:	**Bonjour, madame.**
	Hello madam.
Mme Millerioux:	**Bonjour, madame. Le Figaro et un Télérama.**
	Hello madam. The Figaro and a Télérama.
La marchande de journaux:	**Voilà. Et avec ça ?**
	Here you go. And with that?
Mme Millerioux:	**Avez-vous le Herald ?**
	Do you carry the Herald?
La marchande de journaux:	**Ah non, je regrette.**
	On no, I'm sorry.

1. DIALOGUE ACTIVITY

A. **What does Mme Millerioux buy?**

B. **What did she also want to buy?**

Use the following words and expressions to guide you through the lesson.

VOCABULARY

acheter	to buy	Je regrette...	I'm sorry...
l'argent (m.)	money	le journal	newspaper
bien sûr	of course	le magazine	magazine
la carte téléphonique	prepaid phone card	le paquet de bonbons	packet of candy
la télécarte	phone card (for pay phones)	le plan de la ville	town plan
		Télé Poche	TV listing magazine
la carte postale	postcard	Télérama	TV listing magazine
coûter	to cost	le timbre(-poste)	(postage) stamp
Le Figaro	one of France's leading newspapers		

2. LISTENING ACTIVITY

 How much do the magazines cost? Listen and write down the prices.

Madame:	**Le Télérama, c'est combien?**
La marchande de journaux:	**Un euro soixante.**
Madame:	**Paris Match, ça coûte combien?**
La marchande de journaux:	**Trois euros.**
Madame:	**Marie Claire?**
La marchande de journaux:	**Trois euros.**
Madame:	**Le Figaro?**
La marchande de journaux:	**Un euro vingt.**

3. LISTENING ACTIVITY

 And here are the prices for some newspapers, which are available in France. Write down their prices.

1. **London Times**

2. **Le Monde**

3. **Libération**

DID YOU KNOW?

All euro coins have one common face and one national face specific to each member country. The French motto, *Liberté, Egalité, Fraternité* (Liberty, Equality, Brotherhood) is included on the one and two euro coins that are printed at the Paris Mint.

4. LISTENING ACTIVITY

Listen to Gilles and Sylvie buying some things at the same newsstand. Write down what they buy and how much they have to pay.

Gilles:	**Vous avez un plan de la ville ?**
La marchande de journaux:	**Oui, bien sûr. Un euro cinquante. C'est tout ?**
Gilles:	**Non, un paquet de bonbons.**
La marchande de journaux:	**Ça fait sept euros quarante-cinq.**
Gilles:	**Voilà.**
La marchande de journaux:	**Merci, au revoir.**

La marchande de journaux:	**Bonjour madame, vous désirez ?**
Sylvie:	**Cinq cartes postales s'il vous plaît.**
La marchande de journaux:	**Quatre euros.**
Sylvie:	**Avez-vous des timbres?**
La marchande de journaux:	**Oui.**
Sylvie:	**Alors cinq timbres pour les États-Unis.**
La marchande de journaux:	**C'est tout ?**
Sylvie:	**Avez-vous des télécartes ?**
La marchande de journaux:	**Ah non, je regrette.**
Sylvie:	**Bon, c'est tout.**

What do they buy?

Gilles:

Sylvie:

How much do they pay in total?

Gilles:

Sylvie:

5. SPEAKING ACTIVITY

 Make the requests below, in French, then listen to the audio to check them.

Do you have a map of Paris?

Do you have any telephone cards?

I'd like three postcards and three stamps for the US.

A cola.

I'd like a packet of candy.

6. LISTENING ACTIVITY

 How much do each of the following items cost?

Un coca [ ]   **Les cartes postales** [ ]

Une télécarte

[ ]

Un plan de la ville [ ]   **Le journal** [ ]

PRONUNCIATION

The numbers 60 through 100 are quite difficult to distinguish when spoken quickly. Practice the numbers that occur most frequently: *25, 50, 60, 75, 80, 95, 99...* Listen to the speaker carefully, try to commit the pronunciation to memory and repeat as closely as possible.

Now listen and practice the nasal *n* and *m* sounds:

> *un paquet de bonbons*
> *des timbres*
> *bien sûr*
> *non*
> *cent*

Compare the French pronunciation to the English pronunciation of similar words like *bonbon* and *cent*. Notice that in English, the *n* at the end of these words is pronounced, while in French this sound disappears at the end of a word. Even though you don't necessarily hear it, the *n* heavily influences the vowel that comes before it, causing the vowel to sound extremely nasal (this is because the majority of air in the pronunciation is released through the nose rather than through the mouth as is the case for most other sounds). Listen carefully to the recording again and practice your pronunciation.

LEARNING TIP

French words don't always sound the way they are written. When you read a French word, try to think of the way it sounds, and keep listening to the dialogues to hear the proper pronunciation. You may find it helpful to write down how a word sounds to you, for example:

> *avez-vous = avay-voo*
> *huit = wheat*

When you ask a question in French you end the question on a rising note:

> *Avez-vous des cartes téléphoniques ?*

Record yourself saying new words and phrases aloud. Listen to your recording and compare your accent and intonation with those in the dialogues.

7. WRITING ACTIVITY

Look back at the items and their prices in Activity 6. Write down small exchanges between a newsagent and the following people: *Mme Bidonet, M. Gagnon et Mme Gagnon, Sophie et Vincent.*

Example:

La marchande de journaux: **Bonjour, madame.**

Mme Bidonet: **Bonjour, madame. Vous avez un plan de la ville ?**

La marchande de journaux: **Bien sûr.**

Mme Bidonet: **Ça coûte combien ?**

La marchande de journaux: **Un euro cinquante, Madame.**

Mme Bidonet: **Tenez, un euro cinquante. Merci, Madame. Au revoir.**

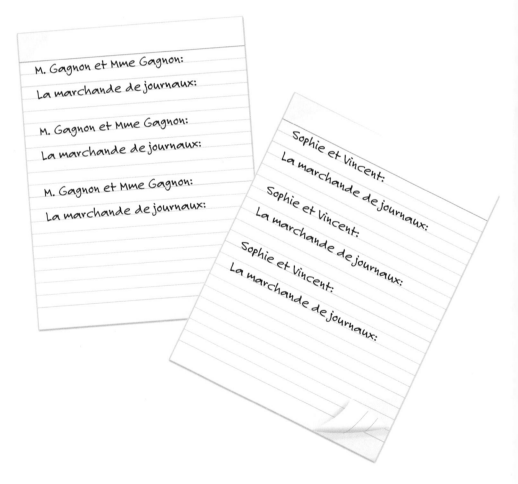

M. Gagnon et Mme Gagnon:

La marchande de journaux:

M. Gagnon et Mme Gagnon:

La marchande de journaux:

M. Gagnon et Mme Gagnon:

La marchande de journaux:

Sophie et Vincent:

La marchande de journaux:

Sophie et Vincent:

La marchande de journaux:

Sophie et Vincent:

La marchande de journaux:

GRAMMAR

Do you remember these grammar points?

If you are asking for one thing, use *un* or *une*:

> *Avez-vous un paquet de bonbons/une carte postale ?*
> Do you have a packet of candy/a postcard?

If you are asking for some/any, use *des*:

> *Avez-vous des cartes postales/des timbres ?*
> Do you have any postcards/stamps?

Remember all nouns in French are either masculine or feminine.

The definite article ("the") and indefinite article ("a") have different forms in French depending on whether the noun is masculine or feminine:

With masculine words: *un journal*   a newspaper
                       le journal   the newspaper

With feminine words: *une carte postale*   a postcard
                       la carte postale   the postcard

Use *l'* before words that begin with a vowel or silent *h*:

> *un hôtel*   a hotel
> *l'hôtel*   the hotel

To make the plural, you usually add *s* to the end of the word, as in English:

> *un plan de la ville*   one town plan
> *deux plans de la ville*   two town plans

But the *s* ending is not pronounced.

Check It!

Test what you've learned in this lesson and review anything you're not sure of.

CAN YOU . . . ?

☐ **ask how much something costs**
Ça coûte combien ?

☐ **say that's all**
C'est tout.

☐ **say how much something costs**
Ça coûte…

☐ **say thank you**
Merci monsieur/madame.

☐ **ask for items at a shop
or a newsstand**
Avez-vous un plan de la ville ?
Avez-vous des cartes postales ?

Learn More

If someone you know is going to a French-speaking country, ask him/her to bring you some bills/checks from restaurants and cafés. Some restaurants and cafés may let patrons take a menu. See how many items you can identify, and practice ordering them.

BERLITZ HOTSPOT

Go to www.berlitzhotspot.com for...

Social Networking
Share your thoughts about what you're learning. If you've traveled to French-speaking countries, tell your Hotspot friends which stores you visited to purchase the different items you wanted.

Podcast 6
Où est le kiosque ?
Download the podcast.

Internet Activity
Search for some large French stores on the internet and access their current catalogues. Flip through and see if you can read aloud some of the prices.

Video 4 – The Money Plate
Did you ever notice the small plate next to the register in some shops in France? When paying for your items, leave your payment on the plate. The shopkeeper will take it, and return any change by placing it on the plate, too. Watch the video to learn more.

Lesson 7 — What's Your Job?

Quel est votre métier ?

Lesson 7 is about jobs. When you have completed this lesson, you'll know how to:

- make introductions
- talk about what you do
- talk about where you work

DIALOGUE

Listen to the game show host asking contestants about their jobs.

Et M. Dubois, que faites-vous dans la vie ? Ah, vous êtes agent de police. Oh là là…il faut faire attention. And M. Dubois, what do you do for a living? Oh, you are a policeman. Oh wow…you've got to be careful.

Bon, et Mme Vernon, vous êtes… ? Coiffeuse…coiffeuse. Très bien, vous travaillez dans un salon ? Oui. OK, and Mrs. Vernon, you are…? A hairdresser, a hairdresser. Very well. You work in a salon? Yes.

Et M. Gaillard, vous êtes… ? Ahh! Homme d'affaires. Vous êtes dans une grande enterprise ? Oui, bien sûr. And M. Gaillard, you are…? Ohh! A businessman. You work in a big company? Yes, of course.

Et…et mademoiselle Leclerc ? Ah, vous êtes médecin…médecin. Et vous travaillez dans un… ? Un centre hospitalier, ah oui. C'est très intéressant. And…and Miss Leclerc? Oh you are a doctor… a doctor. And you work in a…? In a hospital center, oh yes. That is very interesting.

Et M. Maupassant, vous êtes… ? Ah, vous êtes toujours étudiant, mais vous voulez être… ? Comptable…comptable…ah oui. And M. Maupassant, you are…? Oh you are still a student, but you want to become…? An accountant, an accountant…oh yes.

Et..et finalement Mme Beauvoisin vous êtes… ? Ah, vous êtes au chômage. And…and finally Mrs. Beauvoisin you are…? Oh you are unemployed.

1. DIALOGUE ACTIVITY

A. What are the occupations that are mentioned?

B. Where do Mrs. Vernon, M. Gaillard and Miss Leclerc work?

GRAMMAR

Did you notice in the dialogue above that articles weren't included before the professions? When you say what you do for a living, make sure that you don't use an article before the job. For example, *Je suis électricien* means "I am an electrician". *Je suis un electrician* is incorrect.

Use the following words and expressions to
guide you through the lesson.

VOCABULARY

l'agent de police (m.)	police officer
l'agent des postes (m.)	post office worker
l'artiste graphique (m., f.)	graphic artist
l'atelier (m.)	workshop/studio
l'avocat/l'avocate	lawyer
la banque	bank
le bureau	office
le centre hospitalier	hospital complex
le chômage	unemployment
la clinique	clinic
le commerce	commerce
le commissariat de police	central police station
le/la comptable	accountant
le cuisinier/ la cuisinière	cook
dans	in
le dessinateur/ la dessinatrice	illustrator
le directeur/ la directrice	director
le droit	law
l'employé/ l'employée	employee
l'entreprise (f.)	business
l'enseignement (m.)	education
l'étudiant/ l'étudiante	student
faire attention	to be careful
l'hôpital (m.)	hospital
l'hôtellerie (f.)	hotel and catering
l'infirmier/ l'infirmière	nurse

l'informaticien/ l'informaticienne	computer technician
l'informatique (f.)	information technology
l'instituteur/ l'institutrice	elementary school teacher
Je travaille à mon compte.	I am self-employed.
le/la journaliste	journalist
le magasin	shop
le mécanicien la mécanicienne	mechanic
le médecin	doctor
les médias (m.)	the media
le métier	job
mi-temps	part time
la poste	post office
le professeur	teacher
Que faites-vous dans la vie ?	What do you do for a living?
Quel est votre métier ?	What is your job?
les ressources humaines	human resources
le salon de coiffure	hair salon
la santé	health
le/la secrétaire	secretary
les sciences et techniques	science and technology
le/la scientifique	scientist
le secteur automobile	the automobile industry
les télécommunications (f.)	telecommunications
toujours	always/still

69

2. READING ACTIVITY

Look at this list of jobs. Circle the ones that have a special form for the feminine.

m.	f.	
l'agent de police	l'agent de police	policeman/woman
le coiffeur	la coiffeuse	hairdresser
le cuisinier	la cuisinière	cook
le directeur	la directrice	director
l'étudiant	l'étudiante	student
l'homme d'affaires	la femme d'affaires	businessman/woman
l'instituteur	l'institutrice	elementary school teacher
le médecin	le médecin	doctor
le vendeur	la vendeuse	salesperson

GRANMAR

Unlike most French nouns, you cannot tell the gender of the word *journaliste* (journalist) by its ending. Instead, you should look at the article or the context. This is also true for words like *secrétaire* (secretary) and *artiste* (artist).

3. LISTENING ACTIVITY

You meet a group of professionals. Listen to them telling you about their jobs and where they work, then match their names to their job titles and workplaces.

Gilles Bernard	dessinatrice de BD	une entreprise
Sylvie Verlaine	employé de banque	un atelier
Lucienne Briand	infirmière	un hôpital
Patrice Millerioux	directeur des ressources humaines	une banque

Gilles: **Bon, je m'appelle Gilles Bernard et je suis employé de banque. Je travaille dans une banque.**

Sylvie: **Moi je suis Sylvie Verlaine. Je suis infirmière et je travaille dans un hôpital.**

Lucienne: **Je suis Lucienne Briand et je suis dessinatrice de BD. Je travaille dans un atelier.**

Patrice: **Je m'appelle Patrice Millerioux. Je suis directeur des ressources humaines et je travaille dans une grande entreprise.**

4. WRITING ACTIVITY

These people want to join in the conversation but their French is not very good. Can you help them say what they do and where they work? First write down what you think they should say, then listen to Sylvie helping them.

a.   **Carmen Fernandez:**   informaticienne   une entreprise

Je suis [   ] et je travaille dans [   ] .

b.   **Paul Black:**   guide touristique   un bureau de tourisme

Je suis [   ] et je travaille dans [   ] .

c.   **Isabella Rossi:**   vendeuse   un grand magasin

Je suis [   ] et je travaille dans [   ] .

d.   **Jack Nicholls:**   agent de police   un commissariat de police

Je suis [   ] et je travaille dans [   ] .

5. SPEAKING ACTIVITY 66 99

Can you make introductions? See if you can introduce these people. Prepare your text first, then read it aloud, if possible recording yourself so that you can listen to yourself speaking. How's your accent? Check your answers by listening to the audio.

a. **M. Bernard, de Genève en Suisse. Il est** [_____] **et travaille dans**
    bank employee
    [_____] .
    a bank

b. **Mme Rossi, de Rome en Italie. Elle est** [_____] **et travaille dans**
    salesperson
    [_____] .
    a department store

c. **Mlle Verlaine, de Paris. Elle est** [_____] **et travaille dans**
    nurse
    [_____] .
    a hospital

d. **Mme Briand, de Bruxelles, en Belgique. Elle est** [_____] **et**
    illustrator
    travaille dans [_____] .
    a studio

e. **Mlle Fernandez, de Madrid, en Espagne. Elle est** [_____] **et**
    computer technician
    travaille dans [_____] .
    an office

f. **M. Millerioux, de Québec, au Canada. Il est** [_____] **et travaille dans**
    human resources director
    [_____] .
    a big company

g. **M. Black, de Londres, en Angleterre. Il est** [_____] **et travaille dans**
    tourist guide
    [_____] .
    tourist office

6. ACTIVITY

Match the job with the appropriate field.

l'agent des postes	le secteur automobile
l'avocat	la bureautique
le/la comptable	le commerce
le cuisinier/la cuisinière	le droit
l'informaticien/l'informaticienne	l'enseignement
l'infirmier/l'infirmière	l'hôtellerie
le/la journaliste	l'informatique
le mécanicien/la mécanicien	les médias
le professeur	les télécommunications
le/la secrétaire	la santé
le/la scientifique	les sciences et techniques

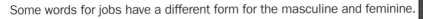

Les métiers   **GRAMMAR**

Some words for jobs have a different form for the masculine and feminine.

a. Words ending in -é add an e:
   un employé (m.)   *une employée (f.)*

b. Words ending in -er change to ère:
   l'infirmier (m.)   *l'infirmière (f.)*
   le boulanger (m.)   *la boulangère (f.)*

c. Words ending in -en change to enne:
   le mécanicien (m.)   *la mécanicienne (f.)*
   l'électricien (m.)   *l'électricienne (f.)*

d. Words ending in -eur: change to ice or euse:
   le facteur (m.)   *la factrice (f.)*
   le coiffeur (m.)   *la coiffeuse (f.)*

7. WRITING ACTIVITY

Which field do you work in? Write down your answer or, if you are not working at the moment, say what field you'd like to work in. Practice saying your answer aloud.

Dans quel secteur travaillez-vous ?

Je travaille dans [   ] .

Dans quel secteur voudriez-vous travailler ?

Je voudrais travailler dans [   ] .

Useful verbs

GRAMMAR

travailler to work

je travaille	*nous travaillons*
tu travailles	*vous travaillez*
il travaille	*ils travaillent*
elle travaille	*elles travaillent*

Travailler is a regular *-er* verb. Most verbs which end in *-er* take the same endings. All conjugations of the *-er* verb sound the same except the *nous* and *vous* forms.

faire to do

je fais	*nous faisons*
tu fais	*vous faites*
il fait	*ils font*
elle fait	*elles font*

Faire is an irregular verb. You should learn the expressions you are going to need most:

Que faites-vous?	What do you do?/What are you doing?
je fais	I do/I am doing
il/elle fait	(s)he does/is doing

PRONUNCIATION

 Listen to the conjugations of *travailler* and *faire*. Practice saying them aloud and use them in your daily life.

8. WRITING ACTIVITY

Translate the following sentences into French and practice reading them aloud.

1.
Sophie and Mélanie are from Nice. They are designers and work in a workshop.

2.
M. Frank and Miss Gray are from the New York. They are tourist guides and work at the tourist office.

3.
You (informal) are from Rome. You are a nurse and you work in a hospital.

4.
We are from Paris. We are bank employees and work in a bank.

5.
You (formal) are from Geneva. You are a policeman and work in a police station.

Check It!

Test what you've learned in this lesson and review anything you're not sure of.

CAN YOU . . . ?

☐ **say what job you do**
Je suis employé/employée de banque.
Je suis médecin.
Je suis étudiant/étudiante.

☐ **say where you work**
Je travaille dans une banque.
Je travaille dans un bureau.
Je travaille dans un hôpital.

☐ **say what someone else does**
Il est coiffeur.
Elle est scientifique.

☐ **say where he/she works**
Il travaille dans un salon.
Elle travaille dans un hôpital.

☐ **say in which field you work**
Je travaille dans le commerce.
Je travaille dans l'enseignement.

☐ **say in which field you would like to work**
Je voudrais travailler dans une banque.
Je voudrais travailler dans une entreprise.

BERLITZ HOTSPOT   Go to www.berlitzhotspot.com for...

Social Networking
Tell your Hotspot friends what your profession is and in which city and country you work.

Podcast 7
Qu'est-ce que vous faites dans la vie ?
Download the podcast.

Internet Activity
Search for *offres de travail* on the internet or go to **Berlitz Hotspot** for suggestions. Browse the different lines of work. How many new words can you recognize? Try creating some sentences based on your new vocabulary.

Lesson 8

A Picture of My Family

Une photo de ma famille

LESSON OBJECTIVES

Lesson 8 is about family life. When you have completed this lesson, you'll know how to:

- talk about marital status
- talk about family relationships
- talk about people's age

DIALOGUE

Listen to each of these people telling Sylvie how old they are and whether they are married or single.

Sylvie:	**Gilles, quel âge avez-vous ?** Gilles, how old are you?
Gilles:	**J'ai trente-deux ans.** I am 32 years old.
Sylvie:	**Vous êtes marié ?** Are you married?
Gilles:	**Ah non, je suis divorcé.** Oh no, I am divorced.

Sylvie:	**Et vous, Isabella?** And you Isabella?
Isabella:	**J'ai trente-cinq ans et je suis mariée.** I am 35 years old and I am married.
Sylvie:	**Avez-vous des enfants ?** Do you have children?
Isabella:	**Oui, un fils de six ans.** Yes, a six-year-old son.

Sylvie:	**Et vous, Paul ?** And you Paul?
Paul:	**Je suis célibataire et j'ai vingt-huit ans.** I am single and I am 28 years old.

Sylvie:	**Et Jack ?** And Jack?
Jack:	**J'ai trente-six ans et je suis séparé de ma femme.** I am 36 years old and I am separated from my wife.

Sylvie:	**Et Lucienne ?** And Lucienne?
Lucienne:	**Je suis mariée, j'ai deux enfants et j'ai trente-trois ans.** I am married, I have two children, and I am 33 years old.

Sylvie:	**Carmen ?**
Carmen:	**J'ai vingt-huit ans et je suis célibataire.** I am 28 years old and I am single.

Sylvie:	**Patrice ?**
Patrice:	**Je suis marié et j'ai deux enfants. J'ai trente-deux ans.** I am married and I have two children. I am 32 years old.
Sylvie:	**Et moi, j'ai vingt-quatre ans et je suis célibataire.** And I'm 24 years old and I am single.

Use the following words and expressions to guide you through the lesson.

VOCABULARY

à côté de	beside (lit: on the side of)	**la femme**	wife
à droite	on the right	**la fille**	daughter
à gauche	on the left	**le fils**	son
l'âge (m.)	age	**le frère**	brother
à la maison	at home	**les grands-parents**	grandparents
l'ami/l'amie	friend	**le mari**	husband
au bord de la mer	at the seaside	**marié/mariée**	married
célibataire	single	**la mère**	mother
le conjoint/ la conjointe	partner	**pacsé/pacsée**	in a civil union
le demi-frère	half-brother	**les parents**	parents
la demi-sœur	half-sister	**le père**	father
devant la maison	in front of the house	**le petit ami/ la petite amie**	boyfriend/ girlfriend
divorcé/divorcée	divorced	**puis**	then
l'enfant	child	**Que... ?**	What... ?
entre	between	**quel/quelle**	what/which
en vacances	on vacation	**séparé/séparée**	separated
		la sœur	sister

1. DIALOGUE ACTIVITY

A. Who is the youngest member of the group?

B. Who is the oldest member of the group?

2. LISTENING ACTIVITY

 Listen again to Sylvie talking with the others. Beside each name below, write the person's age and the appropriate letter to indicate their marital status.

célibataire (C)	single
divorcé/divorcée (D)	divorced
marié/mariée (M)	married
séparé/séparée (S)	separated

a. Gilles Bernard

b. Isabella Rossi

c. Paul Black

d. Jack Nicholls

e. Lucienne Briand

f. Carmen Fernandez

DID YOU KNOW?

 In France a résumé is called a *CV* (curriculum vitae), and includes a picture as well as personal information such as your date of birth, and whether you are married or single.

g. Patrice Millerioux

h. Sylvie Verlaine

3. SPEAKING ACTIVITY

Quel âge avez-vous ? How old are you? Answer the question and practice giving your marital status, whether you have a boyfriend/girlfriend and whether or not you have children.

Example: **J'ai 34 ans. Je suis mariée et j'ai deux enfants:
une fille de 4 ans et un fils de 5 mois.**

4. SPEAKING ACTIVITY

You are having a phone conversation with a French-speaking friend who is curious to know about the people in the group. Review your answers for Activity 2 and then listen to and answer her questions:

Amie: **Gilles Bernard est marié ?**

Vous:

Amie: **Isabella, elle est célibataire ?**

Vous:

Amie: **Paul est célibataire ?**

Vous:

Amie: **Jack est marié ?**

Vous:

Amie: **Et Lucienne, elle est mariée ?**

Vous:

Amie: **Et Carmen ?**

Vous:

Amie: **Patrice est divorcé ?**

Vous:

Amie: **Et Sylvie aussi ?**

Vous:

5. LISTENING ACTIVITY

 Listen to Andre talking about a photograph of his family. Label each person in the picture with his or her family relationship and name.

Bon, à droite, c'est mon fils Didier…et à côté, ça, c'est mon père, Jean-Claude. Oui et puis là, à côté de mon père, c'est ma mère, Murielle. Et voici ma fille Élodie, entre mon fils et ma femme. Là, c'est ma femme, Véronique, et puis me voilà. Et à gauche, le chien, qui s'appelle Samuel, ou Sam.

ma femme	ma mère	mon père	mon fils	ma fille	mon chien	moi
Murielle	Andre	Véronique	Samuel	Didier	Jean-Claude	Elodie

6. LISTENING ACTIVITY

 Ils/Elles ont quel âge ? How old are they? Now listen to Andre telling you how old everyone is. Write each person's age next to his or her name, above.

Patrice: **Mon fils Didier a quatre ans. Ma mère a cinquante et un ans. Mon père a cinquante-cinq ans. Et ma fille Élodie a deux ans. Ma femme a trente ans et moi, j'ai trente-deux ans.**

7. LISTENING ACTIVITY

Listen to Sylvie and Thierry talking about their family photos. Put an S below the photos belonging to Sylvie and a T below those belonging to Thierry.

Thierry: **Nous voilà en vacances; on est au bord de la mer. Ma femme, mes deux filles et le chien, et regarde! C'est devant la maison de mes parents. C'est ma femme, mon frère Denis, les filles et le chien.**

Sylvie: **Ici, c'est mon petit ami. Il s'appelle Auban, il a vingt-six ans…et voilà…et ça c'est à la maison: mes parents, Auban, mon frère Paul et ma soeur Cécile.**

A

B

C

D

8. READING ACTIVITY

Read Lucile's description of a family photo. Draw the photo and include the information that she shares for each family member.

Ma famille! Bon, à droite, c'est mon frère Daniel. Daniel est étudiant et il a vingt-deux ans. À côté de Daniel, il y a mon père, Jean-Christophe. Mon père est avocat et il a 55 ans. Et puis là, à côté de mon père, c'est ma mère, Claire. Ma mère est Belge, de Bruxelles. Elle a 52 ans. Entre mon père et ma mère, il y a le chien, qui s'appelle simplement "Chien." Là, à côté de ma mère, c'est ma soeur, Véro, qui a vingt ans. Elle, comme Daniel, est étudiante. Et puis me voilà, à gauche là.

9. WRITING ACTIVITY

See if you can find some pictures of your family. Write out who each family member is and state their age, taking care to use the right form of *mon, ma,* and *mes.*

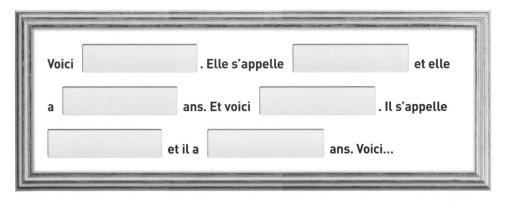

Voici _____ . Elle s'appelle _____ et elle

a _____ ans. Et voici _____ . Il s'appelle

_____ et il a _____ ans. Voici...

PRONUNCIATION

When saying *p* and *t* keep your lips tighter than you do when speaking English. There should be no burst of air, like the burst you get for the first *p* in the word "paper." Say it aloud and notice that there is a puff of air after the first *p*, but not the second. French *p*'s are more like the second *p* in "paper." Listen and practice saying: *mon petit ami; ma petite amie; son petit ami; sa petite amie.*

When asking a question in French, notice how the voice rises at the end of the question, and when making a statement the voice falls at the end of the sentence.

Listen carefully and repeat these phrases:

Ça va ?	*Il a vingt ans.*
Ça va bien, merci.	*Avez-vous une photo de votre femme ?*
Il a quel âge ?	*Oui, j'ai une photo de ma famille.*

GRAMMAR

Possession

You already know that all nouns in French are masculine or feminine.

Just as the words for "the" and "a" change to agree with the noun they precede (*le/la* or *un/une*), so do the words for "my," "his," "her" and "its."

m.	*mon mari*	my husband
	son fils	his/her son
f.	*ma femme*	my wife
	sa fille	his/her daughter
pl.	*mes enfants*	my children
	ses parents	his/her parents

Before feminine nouns that begin with a vowel, you use *mon* and *son*, to indicate "my" or "his/her/its":

mon ami my (male) friend/*mon amie* my (female) friend
son ami his or her (male) friend/*son amie* his or her (female) friend

Note that when spoken these pairs sound the same!

This change, however, does not occur when the following word begins with a consonant:

mon ami my (male) friend/*mon amie* my (female) friend
mon petit ami my boyfriend/*ma petite amie* my girlfriend

Check It!

Test what you've learned in this lesson and review anything you're not sure of.

CAN YOU . . . ?

☐ **say what your marital status is**
Je suis célibataire.
Je suis marié/mariée.
Je suis séparé/séparée.
Je suis divorcé/divorcée.
Je suis pacsé/pacsée.

☐ **say who the members of your family are as if showing photos**
Voici mon père.
À côté c'est ma mère.

☐ **state people's names**
Il s'appelle Daniel.
Elle s'appelle Véro.

☐ **say how old people are**
Il a soixante ans.
Elle a soixante-deux ans.

 BERLITZ HOTSPOT   Go to www.berlitzhotspot.com for...

 Social Networking
Tell your Hotspot friends about you and your family. How old are you? Do you have any brothers or sisters? How old are they and where do you and your siblings live?

 Podcast 8
La vie en famille
Download the podcast.

Internet Activity
Search for some family photos on the internet. Make up stories about the people in the pictures, using vocabulary that you have learned in this section. Try to incorporate vocabulary from previous sections as well about where people are from or where they live, for example.

Qu'est-ce qu'on va faire ?

LESSON OBJECTIVES

Lesson 9 is about what you are going to do. When you have completed this lesson, you'll know how to:

- talk about what you are or someone else is going to do
- suggest things to do

DIALOGUE

 Sylvie and Hervé are deciding what to do this evening. Listen to Sylvie's suggestions.

Hervé: **Qu'est-ce qu'on va faire ce soir ?**
What shall we do tonight?

Sylvie: **On pourrait aller au restaurant.**
We could go to a restaurant.

Hervé: **Ah non !**
Oh no!

Sylvie: **Ou bien aller en boîte, aller danser.**
Or go dancing in a night club.

Hervé: **Non, je suis fatigué.**
No, I'm tired.

Sylvie: **Ou bien aller au cinéma.**
Or go to the movies.

Hervé: **Non non!**
No no!

Sylvie: **On pourrait faire une promenade le long des Champs-Élysées.**
We could go for a walk along the Champs-Élysées.

Hervé: **Oui, bonne idée.**
Yes, good idea.

1. DIALOGUE ACTIVITY

A. What are some of Sylvie's suggestions?

B. What idea does Hervé agree to?

DID YOU KNOW?

 To understand the use of gestures—either to accompany or replace the spoken word—is to know an essential element of culture.

The French repertoire of gestures is extensive, varied and highly original. Learn to pay attention to body language and movement.

For example, using an index finger to pull down the lower eyelid is to say, *Mon œil !* or "My eye!", literally, but figuratively, "I don't believe you!"

Use the following words and expressions to guide you through the lesson.

VOCABULARY

aller	to go	manger	to eat
le bar	bar	le musée	museum
la boîte (de nuit)	night club	On pourrait aller…	We could go…
boire	to drink	ou bien	or (indeed)
Bonne idée !	Good idea!	Oui, c'est vrai.	Yes, that's right/true.
Bonne soirée !	Have a nice evening!	la piscine	swimming pool
le cinéma	movies	Qu'est-ce qu'on va faire ce soir ?	What shall we do this evening?
danser	to dance	le restaurant	restaurant
faire une promenade	to go for a walk	rester	to stay
fatigué/fatiguée	tired	le théâtre	theater
Je ne sais pas.	I don't know.	le tour	tour
Je ne veux pas…	I don't want to…	venir	to come
Je vais…	I'm going to…	la ville	town
le long de	along	visiter	to visit
le lit	bed		

2. LISTENING ACTIVITY

 What does everyone decide to do? Listen to the conversation and match the names to the activities they've chosen.

a.	Gilles Bernard	_____	va aller au cinéma
b.	Mme Fourrier	_____	va aller au lit
c.	M. Delafin	_____	va rester au bar et boire une bière
d.	Sylvie Verlaine	_____	va faire une promenade en ville
e.	Mme Coulot	_____	va aller danser
f.	M. Garnier	_____	va aller au restaurant
g.	Patrice Millerioux	_____	va aller en boîte de nuit

Gilles: Bon, qu'est-ce qu'on va faire ? Moi, je vais en boîte; je vais aller danser. Et vous Mme Fourrier, qu'est-ce que vous allez faire ?

Mme Fourrier: Je vais aller au restaurant, je vais manger. Que faites-vous ce soir, M. Delafin ?

M. Delafin: Ben, je vais visiter la ville, faire une promenade en ville. Et vous, Sylvie ?

Sylvie: Je vais avec Gilles en boîte. Et vous Mme Coulot ? Qu'est-ce que vous allez faire ?

Mme Coulot: Je vais aller au lit. Je suis fatiguée. Que faites vous M. Garnier ?

M. Garnier: Moi, je vais aller au cinéma. Vous venez avec moi, Patrice ?

Patrice: Non merci. Je vais rester au bar boire une bière.

3. WRITING ACTIVITY

Listen to the audio for Activity 2 again. The tour guide, M. Martin, wants to know what everyone is going to do. Write down what you would say to tell him, then practice reading it aloud.

Gilles Bernard

Mme Fourrier

M. Delafin

Sylvie Verlaine

Mme Coulot

M. Garnier

Patrice Millerioux

LEARNING TIP

Practice is very important when learning a language. Listen regularly to the recording and always say the French aloud when you are asked to speak. If you feel self-conscious try putting your hands over your ears. This will help you to hear your own voice better and you will not need to speak so loudly. If possible, record some sentences and play them back to hear how you sound, but don't be discouraged—everybody thinks they sound awful!

4. SPEAKING ACTIVITY ❝❞

Has M. Martin understood you correctly? Listen and answer his questions.

M. Martin: **Patrice va aller au cinéma ?**

Vous:

M. Martin: **Mme Fourrier va visiter la ville ?**

Vous:

M. Martin: **M. Delafin va faire une promenade en ville ?**

Vous:

M. Martin: **Sylvie va aller à la piscine ?**

Vous:

M. Martin: **Mme Coulot va aller au lit ?**

Vous:

M. Martin: **M. Garnier va aller au restaurant ?**

Vous:

M. Martin: **Et Gilles va aller au cinéma aussi ?**

Vous:

M. Martin: **Très bien. Bonne soirée.**

5. SPEAKING ACTIVITY ❝❞

Et vous, qu'est-ce que vous allez faire ? Now M. Martin is asking you what you are going to do. Answer him.

6. WRITING ACTIVITY

Sylvie has suddenly decided she doesn't feel like going out with Gilles.
By email, suggest five things you could do together, using the vocabulary
you've learned. Then read your suggestions aloud.

ENVOYER   ✖ FERMER

De: amis@france.com

A:

Sujet: Visite !

1.

2.

3.

4.

5.

PRONUNCIATION

The letters *n* and *m* preceded by a vowel create nasal sounds
because they are produced through the nose. Listen carefully to the
pronunciation of *on* and try to copy it as you repeat these phrases:

On va danser.

On va au cinéma.

On va au restaurant.

On va en ville.

GRAMMAR

aller to go

je vais	*nous allons*
tu vas	*vous allez*
il va	*ils vont*
elle va	*elles vont*

Je vais can mean either "I go" or "I am going."

Note that *aller* is an irregular verb.

Aller is also used, as in English, to form the near future, e.g. "I am going to":

Je vais aller au cinéma.	I am going to go to the cinema.
Tu vas aller danser.	You are going to go dancing.
Il va aller à la piscine.	He is going to go to the swimming pool.
On va sortir.	We are going to go out. (lit: One is going to go out.)

On, which typically means "one", is often used when speaking to mean "we." For example, *On est en France* can mean either "One is in France," or "We are in France."

7. WRITING ACTIVITY

Some good French friends of yours sent you an email telling you that they are coming to your town to visit. Reply to their email suggesting some things you could do while they are there (*On pourrait…*), as well as some things you will definitely do (*On va…*).

ENVOYER   FERMER

De: amis@france.com

A:

Sujet: Visite !

Check It!

Test what you've learned in this lesson and review anything you're not sure of.

CAN YOU . . . ?

☐ **talk about what you are going to do**
Je vais aller danser.
Je vais aller au cinéma.
Je vais visiter la ville.

☐ **say what someone else is going to do**
Il va faire une promenade en ville.
Elle va au lit.

☐ **say what two or more are going to do**
On va aller manger.
On va aller au bar.

☐ **suggest what you might do**
On pourrait visiter la ville.
On pourrait aller danser.

☐ **say you don't know**
Je ne sais pas.

Learn More

Turn to the employment advertisements in an online French-language newspaper to see how many of the jobs you recognize. Use clues from the name of the company. Guess what the job title might mean, and check your dictionary.

 BERLITZ HOTSPOT   Go to www.berlitzhotspot.com for...

 Social Networking
Tell your Hotspot friends about about what you might or will do on your next trip.

 Podcast 9
Beautiful Paris
Download the podcast.

 Internet Activity
Imagine you and a friend are planning a trip to France. Look online for information on tourist attractions in a city you would like to visit. Write five sentences about what you could do on your trip.

 Video 5 – My... Eye!
While there are different ways in French to say that you don't believe someone, this gesture is a surefire way to show that you know someone isn't telling the truth. Just take your index finger and pull down the cheek under your eye while saying *Mon œil !* Watch the video to learn more.

1. *Comment ça va ?* Match each photo with the statement that best describes how each person is doing.

1.

   a. Pas mal.

2.

   b. Très bien merci.

3.

   c. Ça ne va pas.

2. *C'est quelle question ?* Match the question and answer.

1.	**Comment vous appelez-vous ?**	**a.**	J'habite aux Etats-Unis.
2.	**Vous habitez où ?**	**b.**	Oui, un peu.
3.	**Vous êtes français ?**	**c.**	Je m'appelle Nicolas.
4.	**Parlez-vous anglais ?**	**d.**	Non, je suis hollandais.

3. Conjugate the verb *aller*.

1. **je**

2. **tu**

3. **il/elle**

4. **nous**

5. **vous**

6. **ils/elles**

4. *Je voudrais…* What would you ask for?

1.	a coffee	a.	un déca
2.	two large coffees with milk	b.	avec du lait
3.	mineral water	c.	l'addition s'il vous plaît
4.	with milk	d.	deux grands crèmes
5.	a decaffeinated coffee	e.	un café
6.	the bill please	f.	de l'eau minérale

5. *Le, la* or *l'*?

1. un hôtel   [ ] hôtel

2. un jus d'orange   [ ] jus d'orange

3. une bière   [ ] bière

4. un sandwich au jambon   [ ] sandwich

5. une omelette au fromage   [ ] omelette

6. une tarte aux pommes   [ ] tarte

7. un verre de vin rouge   [ ] verre

8. une bouteille de vin blanc   [ ] bouteille

6. *Au, à la* or *aux*?

1. **une omelette** [ ] **jambon**

2. **une tarte** [ ] **pommes**

3. **une glace** [ ] **vanille**

4. **un sandwich** [ ] **fromage**

7. *Je suis…* What should each person say?

1. I am a policeman.

2. I am unemployed.

3. I work in education.

4. I am a sales assistant.

5. I am self-employed.

6. I work in information technology.

7. I work in a hospital.

a. **Je suis informaticien/ informaticienne.**

b. **Je suis agent de police.**

c. **Je suis vendeur/vendeuse.**

d. **Je suis au chômage.**

e. **Je travaille à mon compte.**

f. **Je travaille dans un hôpital.**

g. **Je travaille dans l'enseignement.**

8. *Travailler,* to work, is a regular *-er* verb. Can you add the right endings?

Je travaill [ ]   **nous travaill** [ ]

tu travaill [ ]   **vous travaill** [ ]

il/elle travaill [ ]   **ils/elles travaill** [ ]

9. What are the female equivalents of these words?

1. **le mari** [   ]   5. **l'infirmier** [   ]

2. **le frère** [   ]   6. **le boulanger** [   ]

3. **le père** [   ]   7. **l'électricien** [   ]

4. **le fils** [   ]   8. **le coiffeur** [   ]

10. *Mon, ma* or *mes*?

1. [   ] **frère**   5. [   ] **amie**

2. [   ] **femme**   6. [   ] **chien**

3. [   ] **ami**   7. [   ] **sœur**

4. [   ] **enfants**

11. Say "no." Make these statements negative.

1. **Oui, je suis marié/mariée.**

2. **Il habite à Paris.**

3. **Je sais!**

4. **Je travaille à mon compte.**

5. **Je veux aller au cinéma.**

6. **Elle est comptable.**

Lesson 10

Is There a Bank Near Here?

Il y a une banque près d'ici ?

LESSON OBJECTIVES

Lesson 10 is about finding out where things are located. When you have completed this lesson, you'll know how to:

- ask if particular destinations are in the vicinity
- say that an action is necessary

DIALOGUE

 Listen to these people at the hotel reception desk.

Madame: **Il y a une poste près d'ici ?**
Is there a post office nearby?

L'employée: **Oui, à deux minutes.**
Yes, 2 minutes away.

Monsieur: **La gare SNCF est près d'ici ?**
Is the railway station nearby?

L'employée: **Ah non. Il faut prendre le métro.**
No. You have to take the subway.

Madame: **Il y a une pharmacie près d'ici ?**
Is there a drugstore nearby?

L'employée: **Ah non. Il faut prendre un bus.**
No. You have to take a bus.

Madame: **Et il y a un parking ici ?**
And is there a parking lot nearby?

L'employée: **Oui. Il y a un parking à côté de l'hôtel.**
Yes, there is a parking lot next to the hotel.

Monsieur: **Pour aller au cinéma ?**
To get to the movie theater?

L'employée: **Il n'y a pas de cinéma près d'ici. Il faut aller au centre-ville.**
Il y a un bus toutes les dix minutes.
There's no movie theater nearby. You have to go to the center of town.
There is a bus every ten minutes.

Monsieur: **C'est où l'arrêt d'autobus ?**
Where is the bus stop?

L'employée: **En face de l'hôtel.**
Across from the hotel.

Monsieur: **Il y a une banque près d'ici ?**
Is there a bank nearby?

L'employée: **Ah non, mais vous pouvez changer de l'argent ici.**
No, but you can change money here.

Use the following words and expressions to guide you through the lesson.

à côté de	beside/next to	**où**	where
à droite	to the right	**le parking**	parking lot/ car park
à gauche	to the left		
l'arrêt d'autobus (m.)	bus stop	**la place du marché**	marketplace
		la pharmacie	pharmacy
au coin de	on the corner	**la poste**	post office
la banque	bank	**prendre**	to take
le bus	bus	**la rue**	street
le car	coach, bus	**SNCF (la Société Nationale des Chemins de Fer)**	French National Railways
changer de l'argent	to change money		
derrière	behind		
devant	in front of	**la station de métro**	subway station
l'église (f.)	church	**la station de taxi**	taxi stand
en face de	across from	**la station-service**	gas station
la gare	train station	**le supermarché**	supermarket
ici	here	**sur**	on
là-bas	over there	**le taxi**	taxi

1. DIALOGUE ACTIVITY

What are some of the places that the hotel guests ask about?

2. LISTENING ACTIVITY

 Listen to these people at the hotel reception desk again. Write *oui* if the clerk says there is one nearby, and *non* if there isn't.

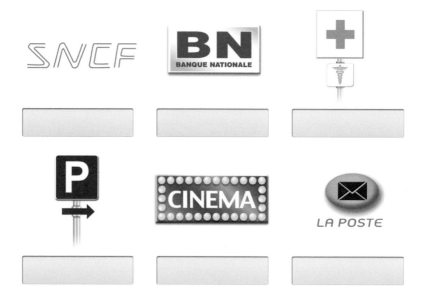

3. LISTENING ACTIVITY

 Listen to these people asking where the nearest subway station is and choose the sketch that matches each exchange.

1. **La station de métro ? C'est là-bas, au coin de la rue.**
2. **La station de métro ? La voilà, devant la poste.**
3. **La station de métro ? Ah oui, c'est tout près, sur votre droite.**
4. **La station de métro ? C'est là-bas, à côté de l'église.**
5. **La station de métro ? Mais la voilà, en face du cinéma.**
6. **La station de métro ? Ah oui, c'est tout près. Ici, sur votre gauche.**

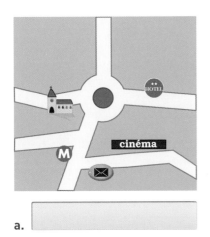

a.

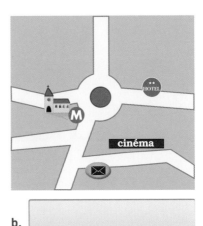

b.

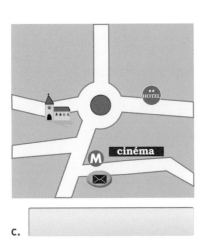

c.

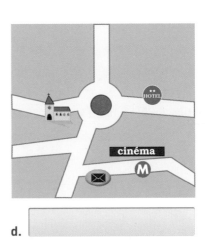

d.

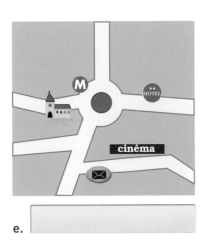

e.

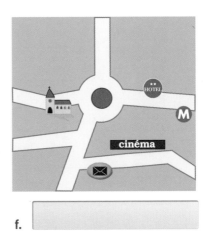

f.

4. LISTENING ACTIVITY

 Now the clerk is telling some hotel guests where to find certain places. Listen to the recording. Then, look at the list of places and put them in their proper location on the map.

supermarché   station de métro   pharmacie   station de taxi   cinéma

Monsieur #1: **Est-ce qu'il y a une banque près d'ici ?**

L'employée: **La banque est à côté du cinéma.**

Monsieur #2: **Il y a une station-service près d'ici ?**

L'employée: **Ah oui, il y a une station-service dans la rue Napoléon Bonaparte, devant le supermarché.**

Madame #1: **Il y a une pharmacie près d'ici ?**

L'employée: **Oui, il y a une pharmacie dans la rue de la Révolution, en face de la poste.**

Madame #2: **Est-ce qu'il y a une station de taxis près d'ici ?**

L'employée: **Oui, dans l'avenue Charles-de-Gaulle, devant l'église.**

Monsieur #3: **Il y a une station de métro près d'ici ?**

L'employée: **Oui, au coin de la rue Napoléon Bonaparte et l'avenue des Chênes.**

5. WRITING ACTIVITY

You are visiting Lucienne in Belgium. From her answers below, can you work out what questions you might have asked her?

A. [   ]

La gare ? Il n'y a pas de gare ici.

B. [   ]

La banque ? Ah non, il faut prendre le bus.

C. [   ]

La poste ? Tout près, à gauche.

D. [   ]

Pour une pharmacie ? Il faut aller en ville.

E. [   ]

Le cinéma est en face de l'hôtel.

6. WRITING ACTIVITY

Now Lucienne is visiting you and has asked you the same questions. How would you answer them? Write out what you would say, then practice saying it aloud.

A. **la gare** [   ]

B. **la banque** [   ]

C. **la poste** [   ]

D. **la pharmacie** [   ]

E. **le cinéma** [   ]

PRONUNCIATION

Here's more practice at making statements and asking questions. Listen to and practice saying these phrases aloud, paying particular attention to the intonation:

Il y a une piscine près d'ici ?   *Il y a une piscine près d'ici.*

La banque est près d'ici ?   *La banque est près d'ici.*

La pharmacie est en face de l'hôtel ?   *La pharmacie est en face de l'hôtel.*

Now practice using *Est-ce que*:

Est-ce qu'il y a une piscine près d'ici ?
Est-ce qu'il y a une banque près d'ici ?
Est-ce qu'il y a une pharmacie près d'ici ?
Est-ce qu'il y a une station de métro près d'ici ?

GRAMMAR

Useful verbs

The easiest way to ask a question is to say the statement with a rising tone:

Il y a une banque près d'ici ?   Is there a bank near here?

Oui, il y a une banque à gauche.   Yes, there's a bank on the left.

Another way is to precede the statement with *Est-ce que* (lit: Is it that...?).

Note that the *que* becomes *qu'* before a vowel:

Est-ce qu'il y a une banque près d'ici ?

Remember: To make a negative statement in French you add *ne* (or *n'* before a vowel) in front of the verb and *pas* after the verb:

Non, il ne va pas au cinéma.   No, he is not going to the cinema.

And in front of *y* when it is included:

Il n'y a pas de pharmacie.   There isn't any drugstore.

GRAMMAR

In French, when you say there isn't something, you add *de* (of/any) after the negative and leave out the word for "the" or "a":

Ah non, il n'y a pas de cinéma.   No, there isn't (any) movie movies.
Je n'ai pas de femme.   I don't have (a) wife.
Il n'y a pas de croissants.   There aren't (any) croissants.

Il faut is a useful impersonal phrase meaning "it is necessary to... ," "you have to... ":

Il faut aller au centre-ville.   You have to go downtown.
Il faut prendre le bus.   You have to take the bus.

7. WRITING ACTIVITY

Practice making the following questions from the dialogue negative. Be sure to make all of the appropriate changes.

1. **Il y a une poste près d'ici ?**

2. **La gare SNCF est près d'ici ?**

3. **Il y a une pharmacie près d'ici ?**

4. **Il y a un parking ici ?**

5. **Il y a une banque près d'ici ?**

Check It!

Test what you've learned in this lesson and review anything you're not sure of.

CAN YOU . . . ?

☐ **ask if ... is in the area**
Il y a une banque près de l'hôtel ?
Il y a une pharmacie près d'ici ?
La station est près d'ici ?

☐ **say that ... is in the area**
Oui, il y a une banque près
de l'hôtel.
Oui, il y a une pharmacie près d'ici.
Oui, la station est près de
la banque.

☐ **say that ... is not in the area**
Non, il n'y a pas de banque près
de l'hôtel.
Non, il n'y a pas de pharmacie
près d'ici.
Non, la station n'est pas près de
la banque.

☐ **say where something is**
La station est en face de l'hôtel.
La banque est à côté de l'hôtel.
La pharmacie est devant l'hôtel.
L'hôtel est à gauche.
L'arrêt d'autobus est à droite.

 BERLITZ HOTSPOT   Go to www.berlitzhotspot.com for...

 Social Networking
Go to **Berlitz Hotspot** and tell us about your town. Is there a subway system? Is there a local bus system? How are places arranged on your street (*à gauche, en face, à côté*)?

 Internet Activity
Are you interested in more practice? Go to **Berlitz Hotspot** to access some city maps of Paris. Practice asking questions like: *Il y a un/une... près d'ici?* and answering them.

 Podcast 10
Les arrondissements de Paris.
Download this podcast.

Lesson 11　How Do You Get to...?

Pour aller à... ?

LESSON OBJECTIVES

Lesson 11 is about asking for and giving directions to a place. When you have completed this lesson, you'll know how to:

- get someone's attention
- ask for and give directions

DIALOGUE

 Listen to these people asking the way.

Pour aller à l'aéroport s'il vous plaît ?

How do you get to the airport, please?

Excusez-moi, pour aller au musée ?

Excuse me, how do you get to the museum?

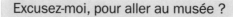

Pour aller à la plage Monsieur, c'est par là ?

Sir, is this the way to the beach?

Pour aller à l'hôtel Mercure, madame, c'est par ici ?

Ma'am, is this the way to the Hotel Mercure?

DID YOU KNOW?

Did you notice the intonation that the speakers use to form their questions? The rising intonation at the end of the phrase is what turns the statement into a question. For example, if you say *C'est par ici* with a rising intonation, it means "Is this the way?" but if you say it with a falling intonation, it means "This is the way." When listening to dialogues and practicing your French, make sure you pay special attention not only to the pronunciation but also to the intonation.

Use the following words and expressions to guide you through the lesson.

l'aéroport (m.)	airport	**l'hypermarché (m.)**	large supermarket
l'autoroute (f.)	highway	**mais**	but
avant	before	**monter**	to climb, go up
la cathédrale	cathedral	**la plage**	beach
continuer	to continue	**le pont**	bridge
descendre	to go down	**le rond point**	traffic circle
Excusez-moi...	Excuse me...	**la rue piétonne**	pedestrian street
le feu	stop light	**traverser**	to cross
la gare routière	bus station		

1. DIALOGUE ACTIVITY

A. What are the places the people want to get to?

B. What is the formula that the speakers use to ask for directions in each case?

2. SPEAKING ACTIVITY

You want to go to a series of places. Can you formulate a question in French asking how to get to each?

1. the bus stop

2. the Hotel Mercure

3. the beach

4. the tourist information office

5. the airport

3. LISTENING ACTIVITY

Which way should these people go? Listen to the directions and choose the corresponding sketch.

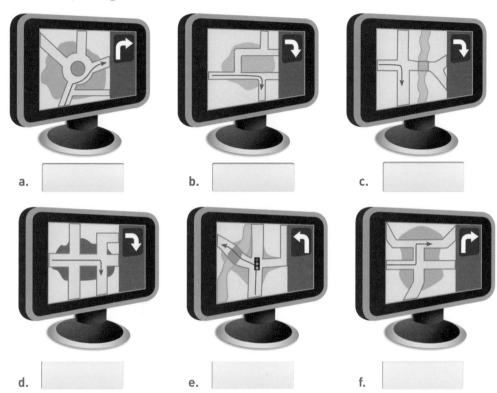

a.

b.

c.

d.

e.

f.

1

Vous allez tout droit et puis tournez à droite.

2

Vous prenez la deuxième rue à droite.

3

Vous prenez la première rue à gauche et puis tournez à droite.

4

Vous allez tout droit jusqu'au feu, et puis tournez à gauche et traversez le pont.

5

Vous allez tout droit jusqu'au rond-point et puis vous prenez la première rue à droite.

6

Vous allez tout droit jusqu'au pont mais vous ne traversez pas le pont.
Vous tournez à droite juste avant le pont.

4. **SPEAKING** **ACTIVITY** 66 99

Say the following English statements in French.

1. You go straight ahead.
2. You turn right.
3. You turn left.
4. You take the first street on the right.
5. You take the second street on the left.
6. You cross the bridge.
7. You go down into town.
8. You go to the light.

5. **WRITING** **ACTIVITY**

Look at the sketches again and try to give the same directions as the speakers in Activity 3. Prepare what you would say first, listen to the audio again to check, then practice reading your directions aloud.

6. WRITING ACTIVITY

Fill in the blanks below using the correct form of *à la*, *au* or *à l'*, then listen to see if you got the answers correct.

a. [____] **banque**

b. [____] **aéroport**

c. [____] **poste**

d. [____] **hôpital**

e. [____] **musée**

f. [____] **hôtel**

g. [____] **plage**

7. SPEAKING ACTIVITY " "

Now draw a small city map, with the places in Activity 6 as locations. Try to include as many of the items in the vocabulary section as you can in your map. Then create mini-dialogues asking for and giving directions to each location.

Un plan de la ville

8. WRITING ACTIVITY

Two French friends will be staying in your home while you are out of town and have sent you an email asking how to get to the following places from your house: *l'église, la poste, la station-service, le supermarché, la banque.* Write a response giving them directions.

PRONUNCIATION

 Listen carefully and repeat these directions to get used to the sound of the *vous* form of the verb:

Vous prenez la première rue à gauche.
Vous allez jusqu'au feu.
Vous tournez à gauche.
Vous traversez le pont.
Vous continuez tout droit.
Vous montez la rue.
Vous descendez la rue piétonne.

Now practice asking how to get to these places in Paris:

à la place de la Concorde
à l'Etoile
au Centre Pompidou
aux Halles

GRAMMAR

Use the *vous* form of the verb when giving directions. The *vous* form of the verb ends in -*ez*. You have already used the *vous* form when asking questions:

Parlez-vous anglais ?	Do you speak English?
Avez-vous des sandwichs ?	Do you have sandwiches?
Êtes-vous marié ?	Are you married?

and in giving instructions:

Parlez plus lentement, s'il vous plaît.   Speak more slowly, please.

When telling someone not to do something you use the usual *ne* (verb) *pas* construction:

Vous ne traversez pas le pont.   You don't cross the bridge.

Remember:

à + la = à la	*Pour aller à la place de la Concorde ?*
à + l' = à l'	*Pour aller à l'Etoile ?*
à + le = au	*Pour aller au Centre Pompidou ?*
à + les = aux	*Pour aller aux Halles ?*

117

Check It!

Test what you've learned in this lesson and review anything you're not sure of.

CAN YOU . . . ?

get someone's attention?
Excusez-moi...

ask for directions
Pour aller au restaurant ?
Pour aller à la gare ?
Pour aller à l'hôpital ?

tell someone to turn right/left
Vous tournez à droite/gauche.

tell someone to go straight ahead
Vous allez tout droit.

tell someone not to do something
Vous ne traversez pas le pont.

BERLITZ HOTSPOT   Go to www.berlitzhotspot.com for...

Social Networking
Share your local culture with your Hotspot friends. What's the most important site to visit in your town? How do you get there from the city center?

Podcast 11
Out and About
Download this podcast.

Internet Activity
Would you like more practice giving directions? Go to **Berlitz Hotspot** to access some tourist maps of Paris. Choose your favorite and practice explaining how to get from one major site to another.

Video 6 – I Have No Clue!
In France, this gesture is used as a way to indicate that you don't know or that you have no clue. It can be useful if someone asks you for directions in a city you don't know very well. And while shrugging usually means, "I don't know" in western cultures, make sure to puff out your cheeks while shrugging to give it that French touch. Watch the video to see how it's done.

Lesson 12

What Time Do You Close?

Vous fermez à quelle heure ?

LESSON OBJECTIVES

Lesson 12 is about opening and closing times. When you have completed this lesson, you'll know how to:

- ask about the opening and closing times of a place
- give the time something opens or closes
- make appointments

DIALOGUE

 Véronique is asking at the hotel reception about opening times. Listen to the receptionist's responses.

Concierge: **La piscine, elle est ouverte tous les jours, sauf le lundi matin et le jeudi soir.**
The pool is open every day except Monday morning and Thursday evening.

Concierge: **La poste, elle est fermée le samedi après-midi et le dimanche.**
The post office is closed on Saturday afternoon and Sunday.

Concierge: **La boulangerie ? Elle est fermée le dimanche après-midi et le lundi.**
The bakery? It's closed on Sunday afternoon and Monday.

Concierge: **Le musée ? Il est ouvert tous les jours, sauf le jeudi et le lundi matin.**
The museum? It's open every day except Thursday and Monday morning.

1. DIALOGUE ACTIVITY

A. **Which places are mentioned?**

B. **Which days does the clerk say the places are closed?**

120

Use the following words and expressions to guide you through the lesson.

VOCABULARY

l'après-midi	afternoon	la salle	room (also used for screen in a multi-cinema complex)
aujourd'hui	today		
Ça ouvre à quelle heure?	What time does it open?	sauf	except
C'est fermé...	It is closed...	le soir	the evening
C'est ouvert...	It is open...	tous les jours	every day (lit: all the days)
demain	tomorrow		
fermer	to close	Vous pouvez avoir rendez-vous à...	You can have an appointment at...
la fermeture du midi	midday closing	les jours de la semaine	the days of the week
les heures d'ouverture	opening times	lundi	Monday
		mardi	Tuesday
Je veux venir à...	I want to come at...	mercredi	Wednesday
les jours de congé	days off	jeudi	Thursday
le matin	the morning	vendredi	Friday
midi	noon	samedi	Saturday
minuit	midnight	dimanche	Sunday
ou bien	or (indeed)		
ouvrir	to open		

DID YOU KNOW?

Though the *Louvre* is perhaps Paris's best known museum around the world, Paris is filled with quality museums and cultural establishments. One such place worth a visit is the *Musée d'Orsay*. Located on the *Rive Gauche*, the *Musée d'Orsay* is located in an old train station originally built for the 1900 *Exposition Universelle* and exhibits mainly French art from 1848 to 1915.

2. LISTENING ACTIVITY

 Now listen to what is said at the reception desk about specific opening times and note the opening and closing times mentioned for each location.

Concierge: **La piscine ? Aujourd'hui elle ouvre à...sept heures trente et elle ferme à vingt et une heures trente.**

Concierge: **La poste ? Aujourd'hui elle ouvre à neuf heures et elle ferme à dix-huit heures.**

Concierge: **La boulangerie ? Aujourd'hui elle ouvre à sept heures et elle ferme à dix-huit heures trente.**

Concierge: **Le musée ? Il ouvre à...attendez je regarde...bon...il ouvre à dix heures quinze et il ferme à dix-sept heures quarante-cinq.**

DID YOU KNOW?

 Did you notice that sometimes the 24-hour clock is used in French? For example, 6:20 p.m. can either be *six heures vingt* or *dix-huit heures vingt*.

3. LISTENING ACTIVITY

 Lucienne is asking the hotel concierge about places where she can eat tonight. Listen and write down when they are open.

Concierge: **Bon, le Coq d'Or aujourd'hui...attendez je regarde...le Coq d'Or... ouvre à dix-huit heures et ferme à minuit. Le Fast Food ouvre à sept heures le matin et ferme à vingt-trois heures. La Brasserie, elle, ouvre à...huit heures et le restaurant Au Poisson Rouge ouvre à onze heures le matin et ferme à vingt-deux heures le soir.**

4. READING ACTIVITY

Clara and Camille feel like going to the movie theater downtown that shows classic French films. Read the dialogue and then write the showtimes on the marquis.

Clara: **Bon, dans la salle A il y a *Jean de Florette* à dix-sept heures trente et vingt et une heures cinquante.**

Camille: **Et puis il y a *Les Visiteurs* dans la salle B à dix-neuf heures quarante et vingt-trois heures dix.**

Clara: **Est-ce que tu veux voir *La Cage Aux Folles* dans la salle C ? Il y a des séances à dix-sept heures quarante-cinq et vingt et une heures vingt.**

Camille: **Ah non... je veux voir *La Belle et la Bête* dans la salle D. Il y a des séances à dix-huit heures cinquante et minuit.**

CINÉMA

A	JEAN DE FLORETTE
B	LES VISITEURS
C	LA CAGE AUX FOLLES
D	LA BELLE ET LA BÊTE

5. SPEAKING ACTIVITY

 Now you have decided you really must get your hair done. Listen and write
down what times are available, then tell the receptionist when you want to go.

**Vous voulez venir aujourd'hui ou demain ? Aujourd'hui,
ah bon. Vous pouvez avoir un rendez-vous à…aujourd'hui,
bon…à dix heures et demie ou bien…onze heures quarante
cinq…ou bien…quatorze heures dix. Et demain, neuf heures
trente, midi, treize heures vingt, quatorze heures quarante
ou bien…seize heures trente. Vous voulez venir demain ?
Bon, à quelle heure ?**

6. SPEAKING ACTIVITY

Some other people have decided that they would like to get their hair done too.
Tell the hairstylist when they want to go using *il veut venir/elle veut venir* and
the 24-hour clock.

Example:

Mme Millerioux veut venir aujourd'hui à onze heures quarante-cinq.

1. M. Briand wants to come at 9:30 a.m. tomorrow.

2. Mme Coulot wants to come today at 2:10 p.m.

3. M. Macintosh wants to come tomorrow at 4:30 p.m.

7. WRITING ACTIVITY

You are preparing a guided tour of the center of your town for a group of French visitors. Draw a map of the area and write an itinerary in French.

Un plan de la ville

Itinéraire

PRONUNCIATION

 Remember: There are pairs of words that are pronounced as a single unit. Listen and repeat these times:

une heure	*sept heures*
deux heures	*huit heures*
trois heures	*neuf heures*
quatre heures	*dix heures*
cinq heures	*onze heures*
six heures	*douze heures*

8. SPEAKING ACTIVITY

Look back at your *itinéraire* and read it aloud, paying careful attention to the way you pronounce the times in particular.

Itinéraire

Telling the time

Quelle heure est-il ?	What time is it?
Il est une heure.	It's 1:00.
Il est une heure et demie.	It's 1:30.
Il est huit heures cinq.	It's 8:05.
Il est huit heures moins cinq.	It's 7:55.
Il est deux heures et quart.	It's 2:15.

In France the 24-hour clock is often used, especially when talking about opening and closing times. You may also hear the 12-hour clock used more informally.

14:30   *quatorze heures trente* OR *deux heures et demie*
17:45   *dix-sept heures quarante-cinq* OR *six heures moins le quart*
19:55   *dix-neuf heures cinquante-cinq* OR *huit heures moins cinq*
22:15   *vingt-deux heures quinze* OR *dix heures et quart*

Remember: In French all nouns are masculine or feminine. The word for "it" is *il* for masculine nouns, *elle* for feminine nouns:

Le cinéma ouvre à dix-huit heures ?
Does the cinema open at 6:00 p.m.?

Oui, il ouvre à dix-huit heures.
Yes, it opens at 6:00 p.m.

La banque ferme à quatorze heures ?
Does the bank close at 2:00 p.m.?

Non, elle ne ferme pas à quatorze heures.
No, it doesn't close at 2:00 p.m.

LEARNING TIP

While you're out driving, cycling or taking the dog for a walk, think about the directions you are taking. Tell yourself where to go (e.g., turn left, go straight ahead) in French.

Check It!

Test what you've learned in this lesson and review anything you're not sure of.

CAN YOU . . . ?

☐ **say the days of the week**
lundi, mardi, mercredi, etc.

☐ **make appointments for people**
Il/elle veut venir à dix-sept heures.

☐ **give opening times**
Il/elle ouvre à neuf heures et ferme
à vingt heures.

Learn More

Pick up some hotel brochures while you're in France. These often give written instructions as well as maps showing how to get there. See how many of the instructions you recognize. At home, collect brochures of tourist attractions near you and see if you could tell a French-speaking visitor about the opening and closing hours.

BERLITZ HOTSPOT   Go to www.berlitzhotspot.com for...

Social Networking
Share your local culture with your Hotspot friends. You've told us what the most important site to visit in your town is, now tell your friends the opening/closing times and days, so they can visit some day!

Podcast 12
Business Hours
Download this podcast.

Internet Activity
Would you like more practice telling time? Go to **Berlitz Hotspot** to access some French movie theater websites. Read the latest releases and the times they are showing aloud.

Lesson 13 · At the Pharmacy

À la pharmacie

LESSON OBJECTIVES

Lesson 13 is about shopping for toiletries. When you have completed this lesson, you'll know how to:

- say that you have forgotten something
- say that you want a particular item

DIALOGUE

 What have these people forgotten to bring?

Lucienne: **J'ai oublié mon sèche-cheveux. Il faut que j'achète un sèche-cheveux.**
I forgot my hairdryer. I have to buy a hairdryer.

Sylvie: **J'ai oublié ma trousse. Il faut que j'achète du shampooing et de l'après-shampooing, une brosse, une brosse à dents, du dentifrice et du déodorant.**
I forgot my toiletry bag. I have to buy some shampoo and conditioner, a hairbrush, a toothbrush, toothpaste, and some deodorant.

Patrice: **Moi aussi j'ai oublié ma trousse. J'ai besoin d'un rasoir, d'une lotion après-rasage, de savon, d'une brosse à dents, de dentifrice et d'un peigne.**
I forgot my toiletry bag as well. I need a razor, an aftershave, some soap, a toothbrush, some toothpaste, and a comb.

Use the following words and expressions to guide you through the lesson.

apporter	to bring	les mouchoirs (m., pl.)	tissues
l'après-shampooing	conditioner	oublier	to forget
avoir besoin de	to need	le peigne	comb
la boîte	box	le pharmacien/ la pharmacienne	pharmacist
la brosse	hairbrush	préférer	to prefer
la brosse à dents	toothbrush	le rasoir	razor
la crème hydratante	moisturizing cream	le savon	soap
la crème solaire	sun cream	le sèche-cheveux (de voyage)	(travel) hair dryer
le dentifrice	toothpaste	les serviettes hygiéniques (f., pl.)	sanitary napkins
le déodorant	deodorant	le shampooing	shampoo
à bille	roll-on	pour les cheveux fins	for fine hair
en spray	spray	pour les cheveux normaux	for normal hair
Il faut que j'achète…	I have to buy…	les tampons	tampons
Ils ont oublié…	They forgot…	la trousse (de toilette)	toiletry bag
J'ai oublié mon/ ma/mes…	I forgot my…		
la lotion après-rasage	aftershave		
les lunettes de soleil (f. pl.)	sunglasses		

1. DIALOGUE ACTIVITY

Name at least one thing each person forgot.

2. LISTENING ACTIVITY

 Listen to the dialogue again and next to each item write the name of the person who needs to buy it.

3. WRITING ACTIVITY

Listen to dialogue once more and see if you can fill in the missing information properly. Pay attention to spelling and accents as necessary.

Lucienne: **J'ai oublié mon** [   ] **. Il faut que**

j'achète un sèche-cheveux.

....

Sylvie: **J'ai oublié ma** [   ] **. Il faut que**

j'achète du [   ] **et de l'après-**

shampooing, une [   ] **, une**

brosse à dents, du [   ] **et du**

[   ] **.**

....

Patrice: **Moi aussi j'ai oublié ma trousse. J'ai besoin d'** [   ] **.**

d'une lotion après-rasage, de [   ]

d'une brosse à dents, de dentifrice et d' [   ] **.**

4. LISTENING ACTIVITY

 Now listen to them buying the things they need and fill in the price tags.

Patrice: **Avez-vous des mouchoirs ?**

Vendeur: **Un paquet ou une boîte ?**

Patrice: **Un paquet s'il vous plaît.**

Vendeur: **Un paquet. Deux euros quatre-vingts.**

Lucienne: **Avez-vous des sèche-cheveux ?**

Vendeur: **Oui, bien sûr. Il y a des sèche-cheveux de voyage, à quinze euros soixante, et des plus grands, à vingt-cinq euros quarante.**

Vendeur: **Vous désirez tout ça ?**

Sylvie: **Oui.**

Vendeur: **Bon, du shampooing, deux euro cinquante; de l'après-shampooing, aussi deux euros cinquante; une brosse, trois euros; une brosse à dents, deux euros quatre-vingts.**

Vendeur: **Et vous Monsieur ? Un rasoir, quatre-vingt centimes; une lotion après-rasage, trois euros cinquante; du savon, un euro; une brosse à dents, deux euros quatre-vingts; du dentifrice, quatre euros vingt; et un peigne, un euro quarante. Ça fait treize euros soixante-dix.**

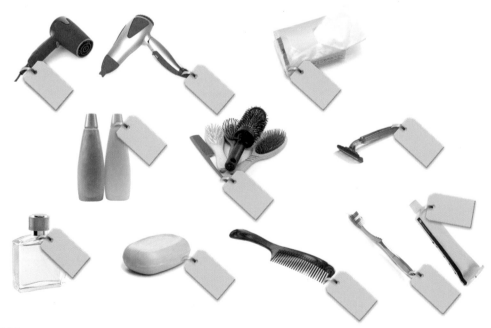

5. SPEAKING ACTIVITY

 Now say what you've forgotten. Write a list and practice reading it aloud, then listen to Sylvie.

Example:

J'ai oublié mon déodorant.

Sylvie: **J'ai oublié mon déodorant,
mon shampooing,
mon après-shampooing,
et mon dentifrice.**

6. WRITING ACTIVITY

Complete the following dialogue using *je voudrais*, I would like, when necessary.

Pharmacienne: **Vous désirez ?**

Vous: [   ] **déodorant.**

Pharmacienne: **En bille ou en spray ?**

Vous: [   ] .

Pharmacienne: **Et avec ça ?**

Vous: [   ] **shampooing.**

Pharmacienne: **Quelle sorte préférez-vous ? Pour les cheveux fins ou normaux ?**

Vous: [   ] .

Pharmacienne: **Et de l'après-shampooing ?**

Vous: [   ] .

Pharmacienne: **C'est tout ?**

Vous: **Non, avez-vous des** [   ] **?**

Pharmacienne: **Un paquet ou une boîte ?**

Vous: [   ] .

135

7. SPEAKING ACTIVITY 66 99

 Now practice the dialogue again, tell the pharmacist what you want.

Pharmacienne: **Vous désirez ?**
What would you like?

Vous: Tell the pharmacist you would like some deodorant.

Pharmacienne: **À bille ou en spray ?**
Roll-on or spray?

Vous: Say: roll-on.

Pharmacienne: **Et avec ça ?**
And with that?

Vous: Say: some shampoo.

Pharmacienne: **Quelle sorte préférez-vous: pour cheveux fins ou normaux ?**
Which kind do you prefer: for thin or normal hair?

Vous: Say: for thin hair.

Pharmacienne: **Et de l'après-shampooing ?** And some conditioner?

Vous: Tell the pharmacist yes, some conditioner.

Pharmacienne: **C'est tout ?** Is that all?

Vous: Say no and ask if they carry toothpaste.

Pharmacienne: **Bien sûr.** Of course.

Vous: You also need tissues. Say: and some tissues.

Pharmacienne: **Un paquet ou une boîte ?** A packet or a box?

Vous: Say: a box.

Pharmacienne: **C'est tout ?** Is that all?

Vous: Tell the pharmacist yes, that's all.

PRONUNCIATION

 Remember: Do not sound the *s* or the *t* at the end of a word, as in *un paquet* or *la lotion après-rasage.*

Practice saying these phrases:

un tube de dentifrice
une bouteille de shampooing
une boîte de mouchoirs

GRAMMAR

Notice the use of *de,* meaning "of," in these expressions:

un tube de dentifrice	a tube of toothpaste
une bouteille de shampooing	a bottle of shampoo
une boîte de mouchoirs	a box of tissues

To say "some" you use *de + le/la/les*

m.	f.	pl.
(de + le) = du	*(de + la) = de la*	*(de + les) = des*
du shampooing	*de la crème*	*des mouchoirs*

If the noun begins with a vowel, use *de l':*

de l'après-shampooing (m.)   *de l'eau (f.)*

137

Check It!

Test what you've learned in this lesson and review anything you're not sure of.

CAN YOU . . . ?

☐ **name items sold at the pharmacy**
un tube de dentifrice
une bouteille de shampooing
une boîte de mouchoirs

☐ **say what you have forgotten**
J'ai oublié mon/ma/mes…

☐ **say you want something**
Je voudrais une brosse à dents.

BERLITZ HOTSPOT   Go to www.berlitzhotspot.com for…

 Social Networking
Have you ever been to a European pharmacy? Did you have any problems getting what you wanted that led to some funny experiences? Share your stories with your Hotspot friends.

 Podcast 13
Les pharmacies françaises
Download this podcast.

 Internet Activity
Are you interested in practicing what you've learned? Go to **Berlitz Hotspot** for a list of links to some French pharmacies and drugstores. Have a look and practice naming items you know and making sentences like *J'ai oublié…* or *Je voudrais…*

Lesson 14 — Can I Help You?

Vous désirez ?

LESSON OBJECTIVES

Lesson 14 is about buying clothes. When you have completed this lesson, you'll know how to:

- talk about clothing
- request sizes and colors
- state your preferences

DIALOGUE

 Listen to these costumers shopping for clothes.

Monsieur #1:	**Avez-vous un pantalon noir, taille 42 ?**
	Do you have a pair of black pants, size 42?
Madame #1:	**Je voudrais un pull rouge, taille moyenne.**
	I would like a red sweater, size medium.
Monsieur #2:	**Je voudrais une chemise blanche, taille 46.**
	I would like a white shirt, size 46.
Madame #2:	**Avez-vous une robe noire, taille 38 ?**
	Do you have a black dress, size 38?
Monsieur #3:	**Je cherche un sweat-shirt pour moi en bleu marine. Je suis grand.**
	I am looking for a navy blue sweatshirt for myself. I am tall.

1. DIALOGUE ACTIVITY

A. What items is each customer looking to buy?

B. What color item does each want to buy?

Use the following words and expressions to
guide you through the lesson.

VOCABULARY

à carreaux	checkered	petit/petite	small
les bas (m., pl.)	stockings	le pull	sweater
branché/branchée	trendy	rayé/rayée	striped
le chemisier	blouse	la robe	dress
la casquette	cap	le sous-vêtement	underwear
le chapeau	hat	le soutien-gorge	bra
les chaussettes (f., pl.)	socks	le sweat-shirt	sweatshirt
les chaussures (f., pl.)	shoes	la taille	size
		le tee-shirt	T-shirt
la chemise	shirt	la veste	jacket
chercher	to look for	les vêtements (m., pl.)	clothes
chic	stylish, smart	les couleurs	colors
chouette	great	beige	beige
l'écharpe (f.)	scarf	blanc/blanche	white
les gants (m., pl.)	gloves	bleu/bleue	blue
grand/grande	big	bleu marine	navy blue
J'aime…	I like…	gris/grise	grey
Je n'ai rien dans votre taille.	I have nothing in your size.	jaune	yellow
Je regrette.	I'm sorry.	marron	brown
la jupe	skirt	noir/noire	black
le manteau	coat	rose	pink
moyen/moyenne	medium	rouge	red
le pantalon	pair of pants	vert/verte	green

2. LISTENING ACTIVITY

Listen to the customers shopping for clothes again. *Qu'est-ce qu'ils cherchent ?* What are they looking for? Fill in the chart with what they want: item, color and size.

Item	Color	Size

3. LISTENING ACTIVITY

Listen and check which item each customer prefers, a or b. What do the customers say about their chosen item?

chouette cool	chic stylish
le couleur color	branché trendy

Madame #1:

Monsieur #1:

Madame #2:

Madame #3:

Monsieur #2:

4. SPEAKING ACTIVITY "99

Have a look at these items. Can you identify them in French?

PRONUNCIATION

 Remember: Some letters at the end of a word are not usually
sounded. However, when the feminine e is added, the letters d, t
and s are sounded. Listen to the difference in pronunciation between the
masculine and feminine forms of these adjectives and then repeat
each one:

grand	grande
petit	petite
blanc	blanche
gris	grise
vert	verte

Adjectives of color come after the noun. Listen and repeat these
phrases to get used to saying the adjective after the noun:

un pantalon blanc	une veste bleue
une robe blanche	une chemise rouge
des pantalons blancs	un pantalon noir
des robes blanches	des chaussettes grises

5. WRITING ACTIVITY

Translate the following to French and then practice saying your answers aloud.

1. **black shoes**

2. **a white bra**

3. **a red dress**

4. **blue and white striped socks**

5. **a gray sweat shirt**

6. SPEAKING ACTIVITY

Look back at the images in Activity 3. *Qu'est-ce que vous préférez ?* Say the item that you prefer in each pair and say what you think of your chosen item, using *Je préfère…* and *C'est…* !

7. WRITING ACTIVITY

Choose something you'd like to buy and then complete the dialogue. Practice saying it out loud.

Vendeuse: **Vous désirez ?**

Vous: **Je voudrais** _____ .

Vendeuse: **Quelle taille ?**

Vous: _____ .

Vendeuse: **Quelle couleur ?**

Vous: _____ .

Vendeuse: **Voilà ! C'est tout ?**

Vous: **Oui, c'est tout.**

8. SPEAKING ACTIVITY 66 99

Now practice the dialogue again and tell the salesperson what you want.

Vous désirez ?

Tell her what you'd like.

Quelle taille ?

Tell her what size you want.

Quelle couleur ?

And what color you had in mind.

Voilà ! C'est tout ?

No, ask her if she has a navy blue sweater.

Quelle taille ?

Tell her what size you want.

Ah non, je regrette. Je n'ai rien dans votre taille.

Respond in your own way.

C'est tout ?

Yes, tell her that's all.

Adjectives

Remember: All nouns in French are masculine or feminine.

In French the adjective always agrees with the noun it describes. Most adjectives add an *e* if the noun is feminine and an *s* if it is plural. Most adjectives come after the noun.

m.	f.	m. pl.	f. pl.
un pantalon noir	*une robe noire*	*des pantalons noirs*	*des robes noires*

Le pantalon is a singular noun in French.

Some adjectives already end in *e* and don't change for the feminine form. They add an *s* for the plural:

un pantalon rouge une robe rouge des pantalons rouges des robes rouges

The word for white—*blanc*—adds an *h* before the *e*. To help you remember think of the girl's name, *Blanche*:

un pantalon blanc	*une robe blanche*
des pantalons blancs	*des robes blanches*

Some common adjectives come in front of the noun, e.g., *petit(e)*, small; *grand(e)*, large:

une petite robe noire	a little black dress
un grand pantalon à carreaux	a pair of large checkered pants

9. WRITING ACTIVITY

Translate the following to French and then repeat your answers aloud.

1. **large black shoes**

2. **a small white bra**

3. **a stylish red dress**

4. **blue and white striped socks**

5. **a trendy gray sweatshirt**

Check It!

Test what you've learned in this lesson and review anything you're not sure of.

CAN YOU . . . ?

☐ **say you prefer a clothing item**
Je préfère le sweat-shirt.

☐ **say what size you want**
Je voudrais la taille 40

☐ **say what color you want**
Je préfère le pull bleu.

☐ **say something is nice**
C'est chouette !

☐ **say something is stylish**
C'est chic !

☐ **say something is trendy**
C'est branché !

☐ **say you like the color**
J'aime la couleur.

 BERLITZ HOTSPOT   Go to www.berlitzhotspot.com for...

 Social Networking
Tell your Hotspot friends what you are wearing today!

 Podcast 14
French Sizing
Download this podcast.

Internet Activity
Are you interested in learning more about French fashion? Go to **Berlitz Hotspot** for links to some French clothing stores. Look through the sites and identify the items you see by item type and description (color, pattern, length, etc.). Say which items you want and what size and color you want them in.

 Video 7 – *Un poil dans la main*
Let's face it—some people are just lazy. In French, the expression *avoir un poil dans la main*, to have a hair in the hand, implies that someone is so lazy that hair has started to grow on his/her hands because they are never used. Watch the video to see how it's done.

À la caisse

DIALOGUE

 Listen to some people making purchases.

1

Vendeur: **Vous payez comment ?**
How are you paying?

Madame: **Avec cette carte de crédit. Voilà.**
With this credit card. Here.

Vendeur: **Merci, madame. Signez ici s'il vous plait.**
Thank you madam. Sign here please.

Madame: **Merci, monsieur.**
Thank you sir.

2

Vendeur: **Vous payez en espèces ?**
Are you paying in cash?

Monsieur: **Vous acceptez les chèques de voyage ?**
Do you take traveler's checks?

Vendeur: **Oui bien sûr.**
Yes of course.

3

Vendeur: **Vous payez comment ?**
How are you paying?

Madame: **En espèces.**
Cash.

Vendeur: **Bon, ça fait vingt-quatre euros quatre-vingt dix-huit.**
OK, it's 24,98€.

1. DIALOGUE ACTIVITY

How does each customer pay?

Use the following words and expressions to
guide you through the lesson.

VOCABULARY

la carte de crédit	credit card	**en coton**	(in) cotton
la carte bancaire	bank card	**en laine**	(in) wool
cher/chère	expensive	**écossais**	plaid
le chèque	check	**les espèces (f., pl.)**	cash
le chèque de voyage	traveler's check	**le jean**	jeans
		large	wide
la cravate	tie	**long/longue**	long
Combien... ?	How much... ?	**parce que**	because
court/courte	short	**payer**	to pay
coûter	to cost	**signer**	to sign
en soie	(in) silk	**trop**	too
en cuir	(in) leather		

2. LISTENING ACTIVITY

Listen to the sales clerk and fill in the price tag for each tie. Listen again to
check your answers.

Vendeuse: **La cravate en soie rose coûte...dix-neuf euros soixante-quinze.**
La cravate en coton rayé vert et blanc coûte...quinze euros.
La cravate en laine écossaise coûte...dix-sept euros soixante-
quinze. Ah ! la cravate en cuir marron coûte...dix-huit euros.

3. LISTENING ACTIVITY

Listen to the dialogue to find out how much these items cost, then fill in the price tags. Practice what you would say to tell a French visitor how much each item costs.

Madame:	**L'écharpe en soie rouge coûte combien ?**
Vendeur:	**Vingt-neuf euros soixante-quinze.**
Madame:	**Et l'écharpe en laine ?**
Vendeur:	**Quatorze euros cinquante.**
Madame:	**Et les gants en cuir ?**
Vendeur:	**Vingt-quatre euros.**
Madame:	**Et les gants en laine ?**
Vendeur:	**Treize euros soixante-quinze.**
Madame:	**Et le chemisier en coton ?**
Vendeur:	**Vingt-neuf euros.**
Madame:	**Et le chemisier en soie ?**
Vendeur:	**Trente-neuf euros soixante-quinze.**

4. LISTENING ACTIVITY

Sylvie is helping you buy some presents. She points out the differences in price. Listen to what she says and complete the sentences below, then listen again to check your answers.

Example: **L'écharpe en soie grise est plus chère que l'écharpe en laine rouge.**

a. **L'écharpe en** ⬚⬚⬚⬚⬚⬚⬚⬚ **est** ⬚⬚⬚⬚⬚⬚⬚⬚
   que l'écharpe en laine.

b. **La chemise en** ⬚⬚⬚⬚⬚⬚⬚⬚ **est** ⬚⬚⬚⬚⬚⬚⬚⬚
   que la chemise en soie.

c. **Les gants en** ⬚⬚⬚⬚⬚⬚⬚⬚ **sont** ⬚⬚⬚⬚⬚⬚⬚⬚
   que les gants en laine.

d. **La cravate en** ⬚⬚⬚⬚⬚⬚⬚⬚ **est** ⬚⬚⬚⬚⬚⬚⬚⬚
   que la cravate en soie rose.

e. **Le pull en** ⬚⬚⬚⬚⬚⬚⬚⬚ **est** ⬚⬚⬚⬚⬚⬚⬚⬚
   que le pull en coton.

L'écharpe en soie est plus chère que l'écharpe en laine. La chemise en coton est moins chère que la chemise en soie. Les gants en cuir sont plus chers que les gants en laine. La cravate en cuir marron est moins chère que la cravate en soie rose. Le pull en laine est plus cher que le pull en coton.

5. WRITING ACTIVITY

You are looking at some more items with Sylvie. Using the prompts given, compare the items, using the construction *plus...que.*

Example:

Le pantalon est plus grand que le jean.

la jupe, le pantalon, le jean, le pull

long/longue, court/courte, cher/chère, petit/petite, grand/grande

6. LISTENING ACTIVITY

Now listen to Sylvie's opinion. Write down what she thinks about each item.

1. **la jupe**

2. **le pull**

3. **le pantalon**

4. **le jean**

7. LISTENING ACTIVITY

 Match the questions with the correct answer, then listen to the dialogue to check your answers.

1.	Vous voulez payer comment ?	
2.	Je peux payer avec une carte de crédit ?	
3.	Avez-vous ce pull en bleu marine ?	
4.	Vous faites quelle taille ?	
5.	Quelle couleur voulez-vous ?	

a.	Quarante.
b.	Non, je regrette, pas en bleu marine.
c.	Noir.
d.	Non, je regrette, on n'accepte pas les cartes.
e.	Avec un chèque de voyage.

PRONUNCIATION

 Listen and repeat theses phrases. Notice the difference in pronunciation between the masculine and feminine forms of the adjective.

Le pull (The sweater); *Il est trop long.* (It's too long.)

Le pantalon (The pants); *Il est trop cher.* (They're too expensive.)

Le manteau (The coat); *Il est trop court.* (It's too short.)

La chemise (The shirt); *Elle est trop longue.* (It's too long.)

La robe (The dress); *Elle est trop chère.* (It's too expensive.)

La veste (The jacket); *Elle est trop courte.* (It's too short.)

GRAMMAR

All nouns are masculine and feminine. To say "it" you use *il* for masculine nouns and *elle* for feminine nouns. With feminine nouns the adjectives must have feminine endings.

m.	f.
Le pantalon bleu.	*La veste noire.*
Il est trop grand.	*Elle est trop grande.*

To say what something is made of, you use *en*:

la veste en cuir	the leather jacket
le pantalon en laine	the wool pants

8. WRITING ACTIVITY

Translate the following statements to French.

1. The wool shirt is too expensive.

2. The leather pants are longer than the white pants.

3. The silk jacket is less expensive than the pink jacket.

4. The cotton sweater is not expensive.

5. The plaid tie is not stylish.

LEARNING TIP

French numbers can be difficult to distinguish when spoken quickly. The numbers 70 through 90 are usually the most difficult. Practice saying the numbers aloud and try to learn the sound of them.

Listen regularly to the dialogues and try to practice speaking French with other learners or French speakers. Find out about French societies or French programs on television or on the Internet. Buy a French magazine or look at one in a library, and see how many words you can already understand.

Check It!

Test what you've learned in this lesson and review anything you're not sure of.

CAN YOU . . . ?

☐ **say how you are going to pay**
avec une carte de crédit
avec une carte bancaire
avec un chèque de voyage
avec un chèque
en espèces

☐ **ask how much something**
C'est combien ?
Ça coûte combien ?

☐ **say what something is made of**
la veste en coton
le pull en laine
la chemise en soie
le pantalon en cuir

☐ **make comparisons**
Le pantalon en cuir est plus cher que le pantalon noir.
La veste en soie est moins chère que la veste rose.
L'écharpe est trop chère.
Le manteau est trop grand.

Learn More

The ability to recognize cognates, or words that have a common original form, will measurably improve your reading skills and help you develop a more extensive vocabulary. You can begin by learning the following French suffixes and their English-language equivalents:

FRENCH		ENGLISH	
té	*liberté*	ty	liberty
	fraternité		fraternity
ment	*seulement*	ly	only
	heureusement		fortunately

 BERLITZ HOTSPOT   Go to www.berlitzhotspot.com for...

 Social Networking
Share your opinions on fashion with your Hotspot friends. Tell them which fashion items you like more than others, using *Je préfère….,* and why, *il/elle est….*

 Podcast 15
Shop Til You Drop
Download this podcast.

 Internet Activity
For more practice using the comparative and stating specifically what you want, return to the links to the French clothing stores at **Berlitz Hotspot**. Look through the catalogues and compare items using the phrases *trop* and *plus…que.*

Video 8 – I've Had Enough!
Sometimes going on vacation can be a tiring experience. If you've "had it up to here" and need a break just place your hand to your forehead and move it the back of your head while saying *J'en ai ras le bol !* Watch the video to see how it's done.

Lesson 16   Off to Work

Au travail

DIALOGUE

 Listen to these young people telling Sylvie how they get to school. Notice that Sylvie uses the *tu* form because she is speaking to teenagers.

1

Sylvie:	**Tu prends le bus pour aller au collège ?** Do you take the bus to go to middle school?
Charlotte:	**Non, j'y vais en voiture. Ma mère me conduit au collège en voiture.** No, I go there by car. My mother drives me to middle school.
Sylvie:	**Tu quittes la maison à quelle heure ?** At what time do you leave home?
Charlotte:	**Ben...je pars à sept heures.** Well, I leave at seven o'clock.
Sylvie:	**Le voyage dure combien de temps ?** How long is the ride?
Charlotte:	**Quarante-cinq minutes.** 45 minutes.

2

Sylvie:	**Tu prends le bus pour aller au collège ?** Do you take the bus to go to middle school?
Laura:	**Oui, je prends le car de ramassage.** Yes, I take the school bus.
Sylvie:	**Tu quittes la maison à quelle heure ?** At what time do you leave home?
Laura:	**Je pars à sept heures et demie.** I leave at 7:30 a.m.
Sylvie:	**Le voyage dure combien de temps ?** How long is the ride?
Laura:	**Quinze minutes.** 15 minutes.

3

Sylvie:	**Tu prends le bus pour aller au collège ?** Do you take the bus to go to middle school?
Manon:	**Non, j'y vais en vélo.** No, I ride my bike.
Sylvie:	**Tu quittes la maison à quelle heure ?** At what time do you leave home?
Manon:	**Je pars à sept heures et quart.** I leave at 7:15 a.m.
Sylvie:	**Le voyage dure combien de temps ?** How long is the ride?
Manon:	**Vingt minutes.** 20 minutes.

DID YOU KNOW?

 In France, a city bus is called a *bus*. A long-distance bus is called a *car*. And a school bus is a *car de ramassage*.

Use the following words and expressions to guide you through the lesson.

VOCABULARY

à peu près	about	le métro	subway
à pied	on foot	faire un sondage	to conduct a survey
arriver	to arrive	Il n'y a pas de problème avec le parking.	There's no problem with parking.
la banlieue	suburbs		
le car de ramassage	school bus		
		la moto	motorcycle
C'est bon pour la santé.	It's good for your health.	prendre	to take
C'est moins cher.	It's less expensive.	quitter	to leave (the house)
C'est plus confortable.	It's more comfortable.	rapide	quick, fast
C'est plus pratique.	It's more practical.	sortir	to go out
C'est plus rapide.	It's faster.	la station	station
C'est rapide.	It's fast.	le train	train
le collège	middle school	le travail	work
Comment allez-vous au travail ?	How do you get to work?	le vélo	bike
		la voiture	car
conduire	to drive	le voyage	trip
durer	to last	y	there
en vélo	by bike	voyager	to travel
en voiture	by car		

---

1. DIALOGUE ACTIVITY

A. How does each girl get to school?

Charlotte:

Laura:

Manon:

B. How long does it take each one?

Charlotte:

Laura:

Manon:

2. LISTENING ACTIVITY

Listen to the dialogue again and match up the person to the time she leaves the house to the mode of transportation.

Charlotte   Laura   Manon

3. SPEAKING ACTIVITY

Sylvie is making some incorrect statements. Use the negative *ne* verb *pas* construction to tell her so and give the correct answer.

1

Sylvie: **Charlotte prend le bus.**

Vous: Tell Sylvie she doesn't go by bus. She goes by car.

2

Sylvie: **Laura quitte la maison à huit heures.**

Vous: No she doesn't. She leaves the house at 7:30 a.m.

3

Sylvie: **Le voyage dure quarante minutes pour Manon.**

Vous: No, the ride isn't 40 minutes for Manon. The ride is 20 minutes.

4. LISTENING ACTIVITY

 Now listen to these people saying how they get to work and how long it takes. Then practice answering the questions yourself. Notice that the interviewer uses the *vous* form because he is talking to adults.

Enquêteur:	**Monsieur, je peux vous poser une question ? Comment allez-vous au travail ?**
Monsieur #1:	**J'y vais en voiture.**
Enquêteur:	**Il vous faut combien de temps ?**
Monsieur #1:	**Vingt minutes.**
Enquêteur:	**Merci.**

Enquêteur:	**Madame, comment allez-vous au travail ?**
Madame #1:	**Ben…je travaille au centre-ville et il n'y a pas de parking, alors je prends le bus.**
Enquêteur:	**Et il vous faut combien de temps ?**
Madame #1:	**Une bonne demi-heure.**
Enquêteur:	**Merci.**

Enquêteur:	**Monsieur, comment allez-vous au travail ?**
Monsieur #2:	**Moi, j'habite en banlieue et je prends le train.**
Enquêteur:	**Et il vous faut combien de temps ?**
Monsieur #2:	**Bon…disons…trois quarts d'heure.**
Enquêteur:	**Merci.**

Enquêteur:	**Madame, comment allez-vous au travail ?**
Madame #2:	**Moi, j'y vais en vélo. C'est plus rapide.**
Enquêteur:	**Et il vous faut combien de temps ?**
Madame #2:	**Dix minutes.**
Enquêteur:	**Merci.**

163

Enquêteur: **Et Monsieur, comment allez-vous au travail ?**

Monsieur #3:   **Je prends le métro.**

Enquêteur: **Et il vous faut combien de temps ?**

Monsieur #3:   **Ben...ça dépend...à peu près quinze minutes.**

Enquêteur: **Madame, comment allez-vous au travail ?**

Madame #3:   **Oh, j'y vais à pied. J'habite dans le coin.**

Enquêteur: **Et il vous faut combien de temps ?**

Madame #3:   **Ben...deux minutes.**

5. WRITING ACTIVITY

Now it's your turn to conduct a survey. What words are missing from the following questions? Use the correct form of the verb in brackets for (a) interviewing an adult and (b) interviewing a child.

a.   **Pour aller au travail ?**

(prendre)   **Vous** [   ] **le bus ?**

(partir)   **Vous** [   ] **à quelle heure ?**

(arriver)   **Vous** [   ] **à quelle heure ?**

b.   **Pour aller au collège ?**

(prendre)   **Tu** [   ] **le car de ramassage ?**

(partir)   **Tu** [   ] **à quelle heure ?**

(arriver)   **Tu** [   ] **à quelle heure ?**

6. **WRITING ACTIVITY**

And you? How do you get to work?
What time do you leave your house?
How long does it take you?

7. **LISTENING ACTIVITY**

Listen to these people discussing the best way to go to work. What do they say about each method of transport? Complete the sentences.

a. **Je préfère** [   ] **parce que** [   ] .

b. **Je préfère** [   ] **parce que** [   ] .

c. **Je préfère** [   ] **parce que** [   ] .

d. **Je préfère** [   ] **parce que** [   ] .

e. **Je préfère** [   ] **parce que** [   ] .

f. **Je préfère** [   ] **parce que** [   ] .

g. **Je préfère** [   ] **parce que** [   ] .

PRONUNCIATION

 Arriver, to arrive, is a regular -*er* verb

j'arrive	*nous arrivons*
tu arrives	*vous arrivez*
il arrive	*ils arrivent*
elle arrive	*elles arrivent*

Partir, to leave, is a regular -*ir* verb

je pars	*nous partons*
tu pars	*vous partez*
il part	*ils partent*
elle part	*elles partent*

Prendre, to take, is an irregular -*re* verb

Notice how the stem changes in the *nous, vous, ils* and *elles* forms:

je prends	*nous prenons*
tu prends	*vous prenez*
il prend	*ils prennent*
elle prend	*elles prennent*

All verbs ending in -*prendre* will follow this pattern, e.g., *apprendre*, to learn; *comprendre*, to understand; *reprendre*, to resume.

8. SPEAKING ACTIVITY

And you? What's your favorite way to get around your city or town? And other cities that you've visited that offer other modes of transportation? Use the structure *Je préfère... parce que....* to formulate your responses.

Tu and vous

There are two ways of saying "you" in French.

Vouvoyer (to call someone *vous*) is the polite form used for people you don't know very well. You will need this form the most.

Tutoyer (to call someone *tu*) is used when talking to children, animals and friends or people you know very well. It is considered bad manners to use the *tu* form in France when addressing another adult unless you have been invited to do so.

Y

Y (pronounced "ee") is used to mean "there" when it refers to a place already mentioned. It comes in front of the verb:

Comment vas-tu au collège ?	J'y vais en voiture.
Comment allez-vous en ville ?	J'y vais en bus.
M. Bernard va au travail à pied ?	Oui, il y va à pied.

Check It!

Test what you've learned in this lesson and review anything you're not sure of.

CAN YOU . . . ?

☐ **say how you travel to work/ school**
J'y vais à pied.
J'y vais en voiture.
Je prends le train.
Je prends le métro.
Je prends le bus.

☐ **say when you leave and what time you arrive**
Je pars à huit heures.
J'arrive à neuf heures.

☐ **say how you prefer to travel**
Je préfère aller…

☐ **say why you prefer to travel in a certain way**
Je préfère aller… parce que…

☐ **say it's faster/cheaper**
C'est plus rapide/moins cher.

BERLITZ HOTSPOT   Go to www.berlitzhotspot.com for…

Social Networking
Do you have any experience using public transportation in a French-speaking country? Tell your Hotspot friends about your experiences and share any handy tips you have.

Internet Activity
Are you interested in more practice regarding public transportation? Go to **Berlitz Hotspot** to access the routes for some tour buses in Paris. Practice making simple sentences with the vocabulary you know using the *tu* and *vous* forms of the verbs *arriver, partir* and *prendre*.

Podcast 16
Moi, le métro.
Download this podcast.

On prend le bus ou le métro ?

Lesson 17 is about using public transportation.
When you have completed this lesson, you'll
know how to:

- ask about travel information
- state your needs and tell others what
  they need

DIALOGUE

Vivian is planning a trip to Paris to visit her friend Anne-Sophie. Read their instant messages as they talk about how to get different places.

Je serai à Paris dans six jours !
In 6 days, I'll be in Paris!

YES! Excellent! **OUI ! Excellent !**

Je veux tout voir ! Commençons par l'Arc de Triomphe. Est-ce qu'il faut prendre le bus ou le métro pour y aller ?
I want to see everything. Let's start with the Arc de Triomphe. Do we have to take the bus or the subway to get there?

I prefer the subway. **Je préfère le metro.**

Quand est-ce qu'il y a un métro ?
When is there a subway?

Often. Every 5 minutes. **Souvent. Toutes les cinq minutes.**

Et pour aller à la Tour Eiffel, le bus ou le métro ?
And to get to the Eiffel Tower, the bus or the subway?

One has to take the bus. **Il faut prendre le bus.**

Il y a un bus tous les combien ?
How often does the bus run?

Every 8 minutes or so. **Toutes les huit minutes plus ou moins.**

Et pour aller aux Halles, il y a un bus ou il faut prendre le métro ?
Is there a bus to get to les Halles or do we have to take the subway?

To go to les Halles, we have to take the subway. **Pour aller aux Halles… il faut prendre le métro.**

Quand est-ce qu'il y a un métro pour aller aux Halles ?
When is there a subway to go to Les Halles?

Every 10 minutes. **Toutes les dix minutes.**

Et Sacré Cœur ? Pour y aller, on peut prendre le bus ?
And Sacré Coeur. To go there, can we take the bus?

Yes, but we can also walk there. It's twenty minutes away from where I live. **Oui, mais on peut y aller à pied aussi. C'est à vingt minutes de chez moi.**

Ah. Bonne idée ! Ah. Good idea!

Use the following words and expressions to guide you through the lesson.

VOCABULARY

le billet	ticket	**Il faut compter...**	It could take... (lit: you have to count)
le carnet	"booklet" of tickets		
C'est bien le bus pour... ?	Is this the right bus for...?	**Il vous faut le 5.**	You need number 5.
C'est direct ?	Is it direct?	**Il y a un bus tous les combien?**	How often does the bus run?
C'est gentil.	That's nice of you.	**la ligne**	line
la correspondance	connection	**Merci.**	Thank you.
de... à	from... to	**Ouais.**	Yeah.
la direction	direction	**Quelle est la ligne ?/**	Which line is it?
l'horaire (m.)	schedule	**C'est quelle ligne ?**	
Il faut changer.	It is necessary to change.	**le ticket**	ticket
Il faut combien de temps?	How long does it take?	**Vous avez besoin de...**	You need to...

1. DIALOGUE ACTIVITY

A. **What are some of the places Vivian wants to visit?**

B. **What are the modes of transport discussed?**

DID YOU KNOW?

Paris holds claim to one of the most dense subway systems in the world. In the city of Paris alone, there are almost 250 stops within an area of under 90 square kilometers.

2. WRITING ACTIVITY

 Listen to Anne-Claire ask the guide which subways to take to four different places. Write down the subway number she should take to each location.

le musée d'Orsay

la Cité des Sciences

le Louvre

les Halles

Anne-Claire:	**Pour aller au musée d'Orsay, c'est quelle ligne ?**
Guide:	**Vous prenez la ligne douze, direction Mairie d'Ivry.**
Anne-Claire:	**Il faut combien de temps ?**
Guide:	**Dix minutes. Vous voulez un horaire?**
Anne-Claire:	**Oui, c'est gentil.**

Anne-Claire:	**Pour aller à la Cité des Sciences, c'est quelle ligne ?**
Guide:	**Ligne sept, direction la Courneuve.**
Anne-Claire:	**Il faut combien de temps ?**
Guide:	**Il faut…vingt minutes. Vous voulez un plan de la ville?**
Anne-Claire:	**Merci.**

Anne-Claire:	**Pour aller au Louvre, c'est quelle ligne ?**
Guide:	**Ligne huit, direction Balard.**
Anne-Claire:	**Il faut combien de temps ?**
Guide:	**Vingt minutes. Vous voulez un horaire ?**
Anne-Claire:	**Oui, merci.**

Anne-Claire:	**Pour aller aux Halles, c'est quelle ligne ?**
Guide:	**Ligne un, direction La Défense.**
Anne-Claire:	**Merci.**

3. **LISTENING ACTIVITY**

Listen to find out whether the following speakers are on the right bus or whether they need to change. Write *oui* or *non* for each conversation.

1. Monsieur: **C'est bien le bus pour l'aéroport Charles de Gaulle ?**

   Madame:

   Monsieur: **C'est direct ?**

   Madame:

2. Madame: **C'est bien le bus pour la Gare du Nord ?**

   Monsieur: _____, **mais il faut changer à la Place de la République, puis vous prenez le quatre.**

3. Madame: **C'est bien le bus pour la Gare de Lyon ?**

   Monsieur: **Ah** _____. **Il vous faut le cinq, et puis il faut changer à Châtelet, et vous prenez le six.**

DID YOU KNOW?

In Paris you use the same tickets for the bus, RER and subway. It is cheaper to buy a *carnet* (booklet), which is a set of ten tickets for the price of seven. There is a map at each bus stop showing the bus route and indicating how many tickets you need for any journey. When you get on the bus you have to *composter* (validate) your ticket by putting it in a machine which stamps the date and time on it. You can also buy a *Paris visite* travel card if you are staying in Paris for one, two, three or five days.

PRONUNCIATION

 Listen and practice saying the names of some of the sights in Paris:

la Tour Eiffel	*le Louvre*
l'Arc de Triomphe	*le Musée d'Orsay*
le Sacré Cœur	*la Cité des Sciences*
Notre-Dame	*les Halles*

Now listen and practice saying some of the names of subway stations:

Château de Vincennes	*Pont de Neuilly*
Porte d'Orléans	*Porte de Clignancourt*

4. LISTENING ACTIVITY

 Listen carefully to the subway routes being described and follow it along on the subway map.

Monsieur:

Pour aller de la Gare du Nord à la Gare de Lyon, vous prenez la direction Porte d'Orléans, et vous changez à Châtelet et prenez la direction Vincennes.

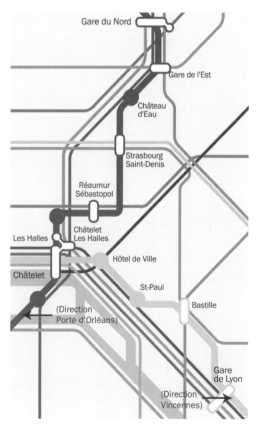

5. WRITING ACTIVITY

Listen to Jean-Claude describing his trip to work. Write down the English translation.

> Le voyage dure une demi-heure. J'y vais en métro. Je pars à sept heures et quart et je vais à la station de métro. Je prends le métro direction Château de Vincennes qui passe toutes les cinq minutes. J'arrive à huit heures moins le quart.

Le trajet journalier (The daily route)

175

6. WRITING ACTIVITY

Listen to these people asking for directions and the answers they receive. Write down the route each person should follow.

1. **Pour aller à la Tour Eiffel ?**

2. **Pour aller à l'Arc de Triomphe ?**

3. **Pour aller au Sacré-Coeur ?**

4. **Pour aller au Louvre ?**

GRAMMAR

To say you need something use *avoir besoin de*:

J'ai besoin d'un plan de la ville. I need a map of the city.

You can also use the construction *Il (vous) faut...*, it is necessary (for you)...

Il vous faut un horaire.   You need a schedule.

Remember: Before masculine nouns *à* changes to *au*:

à + le Louvre = au Louvre

Before nouns beginning with a vowel or silent *h*, *à* becomes *à l'*:

à + l'Arc de Triomphe = à l'Arc de Triomphe

Before plural nouns *à* becomes *aux*:

à + les Halles = aux Halles

Remember: The word for "there" referring to a place already mentioned is *y*. It goes in front of the verb:

Il faut combien de temps pour y aller ?
How long does it take to go there?

In conversation, *on* (one/we) is often used instead of *nous* (we). It is followed by the third person singular (*il/elle form*) of the verb:

We are going to Paris.   *Nous allons à Paris.* OR   *On va à Paris.*

7. WRITING ACTIVITY

Rewrite the following statements in French.

1. **I need a ticket to go to the *Louvre*.**

2. **No, you need a booklet of tickets.**

3. **We are going to the *Musée d'Orsay*.** (in conversation)

4. **How long does it take to get to the *Arc de Triomphe*?**

5. **Is this the right bus to go to *les Halles*?**

Check It!

Test what you've learned in this lesson and review anything you're not sure of.

CAN YOU . . . ?

☐ **ask if you are on the right bus**
C'est bien le bus pour... ?

☐ **ask if it goes directly to your destination**
C'est direct ?

☐ **ask how often the bus runs**
Il y a un bus tous les combien ?

☐ **tell someone which subway to take**
Vous prenez la direction...

☐ **tell someone where to get off the subway**
et descendez à...

☐ **tell someone where he/she has to change**
Il faut changer à...

☐ **say how often something runs**
Toutes les dix minutes.

☐ **say what you need**
J'ai besoin de...

☐ **say what someone else needs**
Il vous faut...

☐ **ask how long it takes to get somewhere**
Il faut combien de temps pour y aller ?

BERLITZ HOTSPOT

Go to www.berlitzhotspot.com for...

 Social Networking
Have you traveled around by train? Do you enjoy taking the train? Or, if you haven't, do you think you would enjoy it? Share your experiences, preferences and plans with your Hotspot friends.

 Podcast 17
All Aboard!
Download this podcast

 Internet Activity
Plan your train trip through France! Go to **Berlitz Hotspot** for a link to the French train system. Type in your preferences: itineraries, schedules, etc., and practice writing an email to a French friend.

 Video 9 – We're Done!
If you want to show someone that it's time to take a break, cross your arms in front of your chest and then bring them down to your sides while saying, *C'est fini !* Watch the video to see how it's done.

Prendre un taxi ou louer une voiture ?

LESSON OBJECTIVES

Lesson 18 is about traveling by taxi or car. When you have completed this lesson, you'll know how to:

- take a taxi
- rent a car

179

DIALOGUE

Listen to these people at the hotel reception asking to book taxis.

1

Monsieur: **Je voudrais un taxi pour aller au théâtre.**
I would like to take a taxi to go to the theater.

Réceptionniste: **Vous le voulez pour quelle heure, monsieur ?** For what time, sir?

Monsieur: **La représentation commence à huit heures.**
The show starts at 8:00 p.m.

Réceptionniste: **Bon, disons à sept heures et quart. Il faut compter une bonne demi-heure à cause des travaux.** OK, let's say at 7:15 p.m.
You'll need a good half hour because of construction.

2

Réceptionniste: **Bonsoir, madame. Je peux vous aider ?** Good evening madam.
Can I help you?

Madame: **Ah oui, je vais au Louvre.** Oh yes, I'm going to the Louvre.

Réceptionniste: **Vous prenez un taxi alors?** So you are taking a taxi?

Madame: **Oui, un taxi.** Yes, a taxi.

Réceptionniste: **Il faut bien compter vingt minutes. Il y a beaucoup de circulation à cette heure-ci.** You'll need a good 20 minutes.
There is a lot of traffic at this time of day.

1. DIALOGUE ACTIVITY

A. Where do they want to go?

B. How long will the trips take?

180

Use the following words and expressions to guide you through the lesson.

à cause des travaux	because of construction	partir	to leave
à cette heure-ci	at this time of day	le permis de conduire	driver's license
aider	to help	la pièce d'identité	identity card
beaucoup de circulation	a lot of traffic	Quand ?	When?
le car	long-distance bus	la représentation	performance (of a play)
C'est loin ?	Is it far?	s'appeler	to be called
la circulation	traffic	le théâtre	theater
conduire	to drive	les travaux	construction
Il pleut.	It's raining.	une heure d'avance	one hour ahead
La représentation commence à...	The perfomance begins at...	le vol	flight
		vouloir	to want
Le vol part à...	The flight leaves at...		
louer	to rent		

2. LISTENING ACTIVITY

 Listen to these other people inquiring about booking a taxi. What is the problem in each case?

1

Réceptionniste: **Monsieur ?**

Monsieur: **Je voudrais un taxi pour aller à la boîte de nuit Aux Étoiles de Nuit.**

Réceptionniste: **C'est sur les Champs-Élysées. Vous pouvez prendre le métro.**

Monsieur: **Ah non, il pleut. Je préfère prendre un taxi.**

Réceptionniste: **Je vais vous appeler un taxi.**

Monsieur: **C'est loin ?**

Réceptionniste: **Ah non, ce n'est pas loin. À dix minutes seulement.**

2

Réceptionniste: **Mademoiselle ?**

Madame: **Je voudrais un taxi pour aller à l'aéroport de Roissy.**

Réceptionniste: **Pour quelle heure ?**

Madame: **Le vol part à quatorze heures trente-cinq.**

Réceptionniste: **Bon, il faut être là avec une heure d'avance….
alors à treize heures trente-cinq. Il vous faut une heure pour y arriver. Alors disons… midi et demie.**

Madame: **C'est cher ?**

Réceptionniste: **Ah oui, c'est cher. Vous pouvez prendre le car.**

3. LISTENING ACTIVITY

Listen again to the last two people looking to book a taxi. Fill in the missing information.

1

Réceptionniste: **Monsieur ?**

Monsieur: **Je voudrais** [_____] **pour aller à la boîte de nuit Aux Étoiles de Nuit.**

Réceptionniste: **C'est sur les Champs-Élysées. Vous pouvez** [_____] **le métro.**

Monsieur: **Ah non,** [_____]**. Je préfère prendre un taxi.**

Réceptionniste: **Je vais vous** [_____] **un taxi.**

Monsieur: **C'est loin ?**

Réceptionniste: **Ah non,** [_____] **À dix minutes seulement.**

. . . .

2

Réceptionniste: **Mademoiselle ?**

Madame: **Je voudrais un taxi pour aller** [_____] **de Roissy.**

Réceptionniste: **Pour quelle heure ?**

Madame: **Le vol part à quatorze heures** [_____]**.**

Réceptionniste: **Bon, il faut être là avec** [_____] **d'avance... alors à treize heures trente-cinq. Il vous faut une heure pour y arriver. Alors disons... midi et demie.**

Madame: **C'est cher ?**

Réceptionniste: **Ah oui,** [_____]**. Vous pouvez prendre le car.**

4. SPEAKING ACTIVITY

Here is the number of the local taxi firm. Pretend you're calling to book a taxi. Prepare what you would say first, then practice saying it aloud.

Radio Taxis 01 12 34 56 78

You want a taxi to go to the airport.

Your flight leaves at 5:45 p.m.

You want to know how long it will take.

You want to know how much it will cost.

5. LISTENING ACTIVITY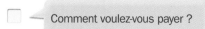

You've decided to rent a car to go to Chartres for the day. Listen to Sylvie making the arrangements. What does the rental agent want to know? Put these questions in the right order.

☐ Vous voulez la voiture pour combien de jours ?

☐ Vous la voulez quand exactement ?

☐ Quelle sorte de voiture voulez-vous ?

☐ Comment vous appelez-vous ?

☐ Votre adresse ?

☐ Pour combien de personnes ?

☐ Comment voulez-vous payer ?

☐ Vous avez votre permis de conduire avec vous ?

LEARNING TIP

When you listen to people speaking your own language you don't always listen carefully to every word they say. You listen only to the key words and your brain "fills in" the rest. When learning a new language your brain doesn't have enough information to fill in for you and you have to listen more carefully.

Listen first for the key words, then listen again and again until you can fill in most of the other words and get the "gist" of what is being said.

6. LISTENING ACTIVITY

Now listen again to Sylvie and put her answers in order.

Sylvie Verlaine.

Hôtel du Parc, rue St-Denis.

Avec une carte de crédit.

De vendredi à lundi.

Trois jours.

Une grande voiture.

Oui, je l'ai ici.

Six personnes.

7. SPEAKING ACTIVITY

Now it's your turn to rent a car. This is the car that you want. How would you explain that you want this car at the car rental?

GRAMMAR

vouloir—to want

je veux	nous voulons
tu veux	vous voulez
il veut	ils veulent
elle veut	elles veulent

Voulez-vous... ?	Do you want to... ?
Que voulez-vous?	What do you want?
Je voudrais...	I would like...

Remember: *On* can be used in conversation to mean "we":

On veut...	We want...

Question words:

Combien ?	How much/how many?
C'est combien ?	How much is it?
Quel/Quelle... ?	What... ?
Quel est votre nom ?	What is your name?
Quelle sorte de voiture ?	What kind of car?
Quand ?	When?
Quand voulez-vous partir ?	When do you want to leave?
Que... ?	What... ?
Que voulez-vous ?	What do you want?
Comment ?	How?
Comment voulez-vous payer ?	How do you want to pay?
Où ?	Where?

PRONUNCIATION

 Listen to the parts of the verb *vouloir*. Which parts of the verb sound the same? Which parts do you think will be the most useful to remember?

je veux	I want
tu veux	you want (sing., inf.)
il veut	he wants
elle veut	she wants
nous voulons	we want
vous voulez	you want (pl., form.)
ils veulent	they want
elles veulent	they want

PRONUNCIATION

Now practice saying the question words.

C'est combien ?	How much is it?
Quel est votre nom ?	What is your name?
Quelle sorte de voiture ?	What kind of car?
Quand voulez-vous partir ?	When do you want to leave?
Que voulez-vous ?	What do you want?
Comment voulez-vous payer ?	How do you want to pay?
Où voulez-vous aller ?	Where do you want to go?

8. WRITING ACTIVITY

Using the question words that you have learned, create a dialogue of you renting a car. Try to incorporate as much of the vocabulary that you have learned as you can.

Vous

Vous

Check It!

Test what you've learned in this lesson and review anything you're not sure of.

CAN YOU . . . ?

☐ **say what time a flight leaves**
Le vol part à...

☐ **ask if it is far**
C'est loin ?

☐ **ask what sort of car (someone is interested in renting)**
Quelle sorte de voiture ?

☐ **ask when someone wants to leave**
Quand voulez-vous partir ?

☐ **ask where someone wants to go**
Où voulez-vous aller ?

☐ **ask how long someone wants a car**
Vous voulez la voiture pour combien de jours ?

Learn More

Look through any French-language newspapers and magazines you have for advertisements, listings for theaters, restaurants, travel agents, etc. Think through what you would say if you were calling to make a reservation.

 BERLITZ HOTSPOT   Go to www.berlitzhotspot.com for...

Social Networking
Have you ever driven in a foreign country? Was it like driving at home or did you run into any problems? Share your experiences and preferences with your Hotspot friends.

 Podcast 18
The Rules of the Road
Download this podcast.

Internet Activity
Want more practice? Use your favorite search engine to access car rental websites in French (search for *location de voiture*). Based on their offers, create dialogues where you rent the car.

1. Vocabulary. Pair up these words.

1.	**l'arrêt d'autobus**	**a.**	gas station
2.	**l'église**	**b.**	town
3.	**la gare**	**c.**	bus stop
4.	**la pharmacie**	**d.**	train station
5.	**la station service**	**e.**	pharmacy
6.	**la ville**	**f.**	church

2. Where? Choose the right answers.

1. **Pour aller à la gare ?**
2. **La piscine est près d'ici ?**
3. **Il y a une poste en face ?**
4. **La pharmacie est loin d'ici ?**
5. **Est-ce qu'il y a un cinéma ?**

a. Ah non, elle est loin.

b. Oui, elle est loin. Il faut aller en ville.

c. Oui, elle est juste en face de l'hôtel.

d. Il n'y a pas de gare ici.

e. Il est tout près, à gauche.

3. *Pour aller… ?* Fill in the correct form: *à la, au* or *à l'*.

1. [   ] **gare**   4. [   ] **parking**

2. [   ] **aéroport**   5. [   ] **cinéma**

3. [   ] **plage**   6. [   ] **hôtel**

4. *Trouvez votre chemin.* Find the right directions.

1. **Vous allez tout droit.**

2. **Vous traversez le pont.**

3. **Vous tournez à droite.**

4. **Vous prenez la première rue à droite.**

5. **Vous tournez à gauche.**

5. *J'ai oublié…* What have you forgotten? Fill in the right form: *mon, ma* or *mes.*

1. [   ] **après-shampooing**   4. [   ] **dentifrice**

2. [   ] **lunettes de soleil** 5. [   ] **mouchoirs**

3. [   ] **brosse à dents**   6. [   ] **sèche-cheveux**

6. *Je voudrais...* I would like... Fill in the correct form: *blanc, blanche, blancs* or *blanches.*

1. **une une chemise**

2. **des chaussettes**

3. **un pull**

4. **une veste**

5. **des gants**

7. What were the questions? Match the question that goes with each answer.

1. **Bonjour. Je voudrais un pull.**

2. **Quarante-deux.**

3. **En noir.**

4. **Oui, c'est tout.**

a. **Quelle taille ?**

b. **Quelle couleur ?**

c. **Que désirez-vous ?**

d. **C'est tout ?**

8. *Il, elle, ils* or *elles*? Fill in the correct form.

1. **Le pull:** _____ **est trop long.**

2. **La veste:** _____ **est trop courte.**

3. **Le pantalon:** _____ **est trop cher.**

4. **Les chemises:** _____ **sont en soie.**

5. **Les sandwichs:** _____ **sont délicieux.**

6. **Monsieur Dubois:** _____ **est grand.**

9. *Tu* or *vous*? Fill in the right form.

1. _____ **prenez le bus ?**

2. _____ **arrives à quelle heure ?**

3. _____ **prends le car de ramassage ?**

4. _____ **allez en ville ?**

5. _____ **pars à quelle heure ?**

6. _____ **vas au cinéma ?**

10. Match the question that goes with each answer.

1. **Le Louvre ? Il faut prendre le bus.**
2. **Ligne 14.**
3. **Non, il faut changer à la place de la République.**
4. **Non, le bus pour l'Opéra est là-bas.**
5. **Toutes les dix minutes.**
6. **Un plan. Oui, le voilà.**

a. **Avez-vous un plan de la ville ?**
b. **C'est bien le bus pour l'Opéra ?**
c. **C'est direct ?**
d. **C'est quelle ligne ?**
e. **Il y a un bus tous les combien ?**
f. **Pour aller au Louvre ?**

11. Fill in the right question word.

1. _____ **sorte de voiture voulez-vous ?**
2. **Pour** _____ **de personnes ?**
3. _____ **voulez-vous partir ?**
4. _____ **voulez-vous ?**
5. _____ **voulez-vous payer ?**
6. _____ **habitez-vous ?**

Answer Key

1. 1. early evening, arriving, 2. the daytime, arriving, 3. later at night, departing, 4. two friends greeting, arriving

2. 1. Mme Renoir bought a baguette and six croissants (une baguette et six croissants)., 2. Mlle Meujot bought two baguettes (deux baguettes)., 3. Mme Duval bought two baguettes and two croissants (deux baguettes et deux croissants).

3. 1. a man, 2. a young woman, 3. a man and a woman, 4. a woman, 5. a mixed group of men and women

4. 1. Ça va, merci, baguette, six croissants, monsieur, Au revoir; 2. Bonsoir, Mademoiselle (Mlle), pas mal, Vous, Deux, Voilà; 3. messieursdames, Très bien, s'il vous plaît, croissants

5. Madame: ✓ (line 3), Monsieur: ✓ (line 4); Mlle Henry: ✓ (line 3), M. Dupont: + (line 4); M. Desart: + (line 3), Mme Simon: + (line 4)

6. Answers will vary.

7. Sample answers: 1. Mme; Très bien, merci; *insert your name*; Mme; 2. Bonsoir; *insert your name*; Oui, ça va; *insert your name*; Au revoir; 3. Bonsoir; *insert your name*; Oui, ça va, Mlle

9. une baguette, baguettes; un boulanger, boulangers; un croissant, croissants; une madame, mesdames; un monsieur, monsieurs

194

LESSON 2

1. Genève, Paris, Bruxelles, Québec; Suisse, France, Belgique, Canada

2. a. Gilles Bernard, Suisse, M. Bernard est suisse.; b. Sylvie Verlaine, France, Mlle Verlaine est française.;
   c. Lucienne Briand, Belgique. Mme Briand est belge.; d. Patrice Millerioux, Canada, M. Millerioux est canadien.

3. Je vous présente Mlle Sylvie Verlaine. Elle est française et elle habite à Paris en France.; Je vous présente Mme Lucienne Briand. Elle est belge et elle habite à Bruxelles en Belgique.; Je vous présente M. Patrice Millerioux. Il est canadien, d'origine française et il habite à Québec.

4. 1. Madame Briand est suisse?, Non, elle n'est pas suisse, elle est belge.; 2. Monsieur Millerioux est anglais?, Non, il n'est pas anglais, il est canadien.

5. a. français, anglais; b. m'appelle, suis, habite, en, de français; c. habite, aux, et, américain; d. au, suis, anglais; e. Rosa, Rio, Brésil, un peu

6. Answers will vary.

7. Sample answer: Vous êtes espagnole?

9. l'Allemagne, l'Angleterre, les Antilles, la Belgique, le Brésil, le Canada, l'Espagne, les États-Unis, la France, l'Italie, le Japon, la Suisse

10. Au: au Brésil, au Canada, au Japon; Aux: aux Antilles, aux États-Unis; En: en Allemagne, en Angleterre, en Belgique, en Espagne, en France, en Italie, en Suisse

11. Je suis japonaise. Je parle japonais.; Je suis italien. Je parle italien.; Je suis belge. Je parle français.; Je suis allemande. Je parle allemand.: Je suis brésilienne. Je parle portugais. Je suis suisse. Je parle français.; Je suis canadien. Je parle anglais.

12. 1. Elles sont Claudia et Paula. Elles sont espagnoles.; 2. Vous êtes Giuseppe. Vous êtes italien.; 3. Il est Timiko. Il est japonais ?; 4. Elle est Gisele. Elle est brésilienne ?; Je suis Alexis. Je suis belge. Je ne suis pas français.

LESSON 3

1. Fernandez, Graham, Macintosh, Rossellini, Schwartz; Comment ça s'écrit?, Pouvez-vous épeler ça?

5. a. 19, b. 13, c. 7, d. 11, e. 9

8. Answers will vary.

LESSON 4

1. M. Albert: un café, Mme Albert: un grand crème, Nathalie: un jus d'orange, Delphine: un chocolat chaud; quatre croissants

2. Je voudrais un café., Un crème pour moi., Grand….et….un jus d'orange pour Nathalie., Je voudrais un chocolat chaud., Quatre croissants, s'il vous plaît.

3. Je voudrais un grand crème., Deux express, s'il vous plaît., Un thé au lait, s'il vous plaît., Deux cafés., Avez-vous des croissants?, Je voudrais un déca., Une bière, s'il vous plaît., Un coca et de l'eau minérale gazeuse.

4. 1. Deux grands crèmes, 2. Un café, un chocolat et deux croissants, 3. Une bière et de l'eau minérale gazeuse, 4. Un jus d'orange et un croissant, 5. Un déca, un grand crème, un thé au lait et deux croissants, 6. Quatre cafés

6. un café, un grand crème, un jus d'orange; 9,20€

1. Madame: un verre de vin rouge, Monsieur: une pression.; Madame: un sandwich au jambon, Monsieur: un sandwich au fromage.

2. s'il vous plaît, sandwichs, Qu'est-ce que vous avez, jambon, fromage, boisson, vin

3. 1. Qu'est-ce que vous avez comme sandwichs ?, 2. Qu'est-ce que vous avez comme salades ?,
   3. Qu'est-ce que vous avez comme glaces ?, 4. Qu'est-ce que vous avez comme omelettes ?,
   5. Qu'est-ce que vous avez comme desserts ?

4. Sample Answers: Je voudrais un milk-shake pour moi et une bière pression pour mon ami. Je voudrais un dessert pour moi et une portion de frites pour mon ami.

5. 1. une salade niçoise et de l'eau minérale gazeuse, 2. un steak frites et un pichet de vin rouge, 3. deux hamburgers, une grande portion de frites, un coca et un milk shake à la vanille, 4. une omelette aux fines herbes, une salade aux fruits de mer, un thé au citron et une bière à pression

6. 1. glace à la fraise, 2.rien (*nothing*), 3. deux tartes aux pommes, 4. tarte au citron et une glace au chocolat

8. …vingt-sept euros; …vingt-neuf euros soixante; …trente-six euros; …vingt-trois euros quarante; …vingt-cinq euros soixante-dix

9. Table une: 14,40€, Table deux: 9€, Table trois 16,50€, Table quatre: 12,60€, Table cinq: 17,70€

LESSON 6

1. Le Figaro et un Télérama; le Herald

2. Le Télérama: un euro soixante (1,60€), Paris Match: trois euros (3€), Marie Claire: trois euros (3€), Le Figaro: un euro vingt (1,20€)

3. 1. London Times: un euro cinquante (1,50€), 2. Le Monde: un euro vingt (1,20€), 3. Libération: un euro (1€)

4. Gilles: un plan de la ville et un paquet de bonbons: sept euros quarante-cinq (7,45€); Sylvie: cinq cartes postales (4€), cinq timbres pour les États-Unis (The price of the stamps is not mentioned.)

5. Avez-vous un plan de Paris?, Avez-vous des télécartes?, Je voudrais trois cartes postales et trois timbres pour les États-Unis., Un coca., Je voudrais un paquet de bonbons.

6. the cola: 2,50€, the post cards: 0,80€, the telephone cards: 7,50€ or 15€, the town map: 1,50€, the newspaper: 1,20€

7. Answers will vary.

8. Answers will vary.

LESSON 7

1. agent de police, coiffeuse, homme d'affaires, médecin, étudiant; Mme Vernon travaille dans un salon,; M. Gaillard travaille dans une grande entreprise.; Mlle Leclerc travaille dans un centre hospitalier.

2. la coiffeuse, la cuisinière, la directrice, l'étudiante, la femme d'affaires, l'institutrice, la vendeuse

3. Gilles Bernard: employé de banque, une banque; Sylvie Verlaine: infirmière, un hôpital; Lucienne Briand: dessinatrice de BD, un atelier; Patrice Millerioux: directeur des ressources humaines, une grande entreprise

4. a. Carmen: Je suis informaticienne et je travaille dans une entreprise.; b. Paul: Je suis guide touristique et je travaille dans un bureau de tourisme.; c. Isabella: Je suis vendeuse et je travaille dans un grand magasin.; d. Jack: Je suis agent de police et je travaille dans un commissariat de police.

5. a. M. Bernard, de Genève en Suisse. Il est employé de banque et travaille dans une banque.; b. Mme Rossi, de Rome en Italie. Elle est vendeuse et travaille dans un grand magasin.; c. Mlle Verlaine, de Paris. Elle est infirmière et travaille dans un hôpital.; d. Mlle Briand, de Bruxelles en Belgique. Elle est dessinatrice de BD et travaille dans un atelier.; e. Mlle Fernandez, de Madrid en Espagne. Elle est informaticienne et travaille dans un bureau.; f. M. Millerioux, de Québec au Canada. Il est directeur des ressources humaines et travaille dans une grande entreprise.; g. M. Black, de Londres en Angleterre. Il est guide touristique et travaille dans un bureau de tourisme.

6. le secteur automobile—le/la mécanicien(ne), le commerce—le/la comptable, le droit—l'avocat, l'enseignement—le professeur, l'hôtellerie—le cuisinier/la cuisinière, l'informatique—l'informaticien(ne), les médias—le/la journaliste, les télécommunications—l'agent des postes, la santé—l'infirmier/l'infirmière, les sciences et techniques—le/la scientifique

7. Answers will vary.

8. 1. Sophie et Mélanie sont de Nice. Elles sont dessinatrices et travaillent dans un atelier.; 2. M. Frank et Mlle Gray sont de New York. Ils sont guides touristique et travaillent dans un bureau de tourisme.;
3. Tu es de Rome. Tu es infirmier/infirmière et travailles dans un hôpital.; 4. Nous sommes de Paris. Nous sommes employés de banque et travaillons dans une banque.: 5. Vous êtes de Genève. Vous êtes agent de police et travaillez dans un commissariat de police.

LESSON 8

1. Sylvie: 24 ans, Jack: 36 ans

2. a. Gilles: 32, D; b. Isabella: 35, M; c. Paul: 28, C; d. Jack: 36, S; e. Lucienne: 33, M; f. Carmen: 28, C; g. Patrice: 32, M; h. Sylvie: 24, C

3. Answers will vary.

4. Non, il est divorcé.; Non, elle est mariée.; Oui, il est célibataire.; Non, il est séparé.; Oui, elle est mariée.; Carmen est célibataire,; Non, il est marié.; Non, elle est célibataire.

5. (from left to right) mon chien, Samuel; ma femme, Véronique; ma fille, Élodie; moi, Patrice; mon fils, Didier; mon père, Jean-Claude; ma mère, Murielle

6. ma femme, Véronique, 30 ans; ma fille, Élodie, 2 ans; moi, Patrice, 32 ans; mon fils, Didier, 4 ans; mon père, Jean-Claude, 55 ans; ma mère, Murielle, 51 ans

7. T: a, c; S: b, d

8. (from left to right) Lucile, Véro (sa soeur, 20 ans, étudiante), Claire (sa mère, 52 ans, de Belgique), le chien "chien," Jean-Christophe (son père, 55 ans, avocat), Daniel (son frère, 22 ans étudiant)

9. Sample Answer: Voici ma mère. Elle s'appelle Anne et elle a soixante ans. Et voici mon père. Il s'appelle Jack et il a soixante-deux ans. Voici ma soeur. Elle s'appelle Marie et elle a vingt-cinq ans….

1. aller au restaurant, aller en boîte, aller danser, aller au cinéma, faire une promenade le long des Champs-Élysées; faire une promenade le long des Champs-Élysées

2. a. Gilles Bernard: va aller danser.; b. Mme Fourrier: va aller au restaurant.; c. M. Delafin: va faire une promenade en ville.; d. Sylvie Verlaine: va aller en boîte de nuit.; e. Mme Coulot: va aller au lit.; f. M. Garnier: va aller au cinéma.; g. Patrice Millerioux: va rester au bar et boire une bière.

3. Gilles Bernard va aller danser.; Mme Fourrier va aller au restaurant.; M. Delafin va faire une promenade en ville.; Sylvie Verlaine va aller en boîte de nuit.; Mme Coulot va aller au lit.; M. Garnier va aller au cinéma.; Patrice Millerioux va rester au bar et boire une bière.

4. Non, il ne va pas aller au cinéma. Il va rester au bar boire une bière.; Non, elle ne va pas visiter la ville. Elle va manger au restaurant.; Oui, c'est vrai.; Non, Sylvie ne va pas aller à la piscine. Elle va aller en boîte de nuit.; Oui, c'est vrai. Elle est fatiguée.; Non, il ne va pas aller au restaurant. Il va aller au cinéma.; Ah non, il ne va pas aller au cinéma. Il va aller en boîte de nuit avec Sylvie.

5. Answers will vary.

6. Answers will vary.

7. Answers will vary.

TEST 1

1. 1. b; 2. a; 3. c

2. 1. c; 2. a; 3. d; 4. b

3. vais; vas; va; allons; allez; vont

4. 1. e; 2. d; 3. f; 4. b; 5. a; 6. c

5. 1. l'; 2. le; 3. la; 4. le; 5. l'; 6. la; 7. le; 8. la

6. 1. au; 2. aux; 3. à la; 4. au

7. 1. b; 2. d; 3. g; 4. c; 5. e; 6. a; 7. f

8. je travaille, tu travailles, il/elle travaille, nous travaillons, vous travaillez, ils/elles travaillent

9. 1. la femme; 2. la sœur; 3. la mère; 4. la fille; 5. l'infirmière; 6. la boulangère; 7. l'électricienne; 8. la coiffeuse

10. 1. mon; 2. ma; 3. mon; 4. mes; 5. mon; 6. mon; 7. ma

11. 1. Non, je ne suis pas marié(e).; 2. Il n'habite pas à Paris.; 3. Je ne sais pas !; 4. Je ne travaille pas à mon compte.; 5. Je ne veux pas aller au cinéma.; 6. Elle n'est pas comptable.

1. une poste, la gare SNCF, une pharmacie, un parking, un cinéma, un arrêt d'autobus, une banque

2. une poste, oui; la gare SNCF, non; une pharmacie, non; un parking, oui; un cinéma, non; un arrêt d'autobus, oui; une banque, non

3. 1. a; 2. c; 3. f; 4. b; 5. d; 6. e

4. La banque est à côté du cinéma., La station service est dans la rue Napoléon Bonaparte devant le supermarché., La pharmacie est dans la rue de la Révolution en face de la poste., La station de taxi est dans l'avenue Charles-de-Gaulle, devant l'église., La station de métro est au coin de la rue Napoléon Bonaparte et l'avenue des Chênes.

5. a. Il y a une gare près d'ici?, b. Est-ce que la banque est près d'ici?, c. La poste est près d'ici?, d. Est-ce qu'il y a une pharmacie près d'ici?, e. Il y a un cinéma près d'ici?

6. a. La gare ? Il n'y a pas de gare ici., b. La banque ? Ah non, il faut prendre le bus., c. La poste ? Tout près, à gauche., d. Pour une pharmacie ? Il faut aller en ville., e. Le cinéma est en face de l'hôtel.

7. 1. Il n'y a pas de poste près d'ici?, 2. La gare SNCF n'est pas près d'ici?, 3. Il n'y a pas de pharmacie près d'ici?, 4. Il n'y a pas de parking ici?, 5. Il n'y a pas de banque près d'ici?

LESSON 11

1. l'aéroport, le musée, la plage, l'autoroute, l'hôtel Mercure; Pour aller à…

2. 1. Pour aller à l'arrêt de bus ? (How do I get to the bus stop ?), Pour aller à l'hôtel Mercure ? (How do I get to the Hotel Mercure?), Pour aller à la plage ? (How do I get to the beach?), Pour aller au musée ? (How do I get to the museum?), Pour aller à l'aéroport ? (How do I get to the airport?)

3. a. 5; b. 1; c. 6; d. 2; e. 4; f. 3

4. 1. Vous allez tout droit., 2. Vous tournez à droite., 3. Vous tournez à gauche., 4. Vous prenez la première rue à droite., 5. Vous prenez la deuxième rue à gauche., 6. Vous traversez le pont., 7. Vous descendez en ville., 8. Vous allez jusqu'au feu.

5. 1. Vous allez tout droit et puis vous tournez à droite., 2. Vous prenez la deuxième rue à droite., 3. Vous prenez la première rue à gauche et puis tournez à droite., 4. Vous allez tout droit jusqu'au feu et puis tournez à gauche et traversex le pont., 5. Vous allez tout droit jusqu'au rond point et puis vous prenez la première rue à droite., 6. Vous allez tout droit jusqu'au pont mais vous ne traversez pas le pont. Vous tournez à droite juste avant le pont.

6. a. à la banque; b. à l'aéroport; c. à la poste; d. à l'hôpital; e. au musée; f. à l'hôtel; g. à la plage

7. Answers will vary.

8. Answers will vary.

9. Answers will vary.

LESSON 12

1. la piscine, la poste, la boulangerie, le musée; La piscine est fermée le lundi matin et le jeudi soir., La poste est fermée le samedi après-midi et le dimanche., La boulangerie est fermée le dimanche après-midi et le lundi., Le musée est fermé le jeudi et le lundi matin.

2. la piscine: 7:30 a.m.-9:30 p.m.; la poste: 9:00 a.m.-6:00 p.m.; la boulangerie: 7:00 a.m.-6:30 p.m.; le musée: 10:15 a.m.-5:45 p.m.

3. le Coq d'Or: 6:00 p.m.-12:00 a.m.; le Fast Food: 7:00 a.m.-11:00 p.m.; la Brasserie: 8:00 a.m.; Au Poisson Rouge: 11:00 a.m.-10:00 p.m.

4. Jean de Florette: 17:30 & 21:50; Les Visiteurs: 19:40 & 23:10; La Cage Aux Folles 17:45 & 21:20; La Belle et la Bête 18:50 & 0:00

5. Answers will vary.

6. 1. M. Briand veut venir demain à neuf heures trente., 2. Mme Coulot veut venir aujourd'hui à quatorze heures dix., 3. M. Macintosh veut venir demain à seize heures trente.

7. Answers will vary.

8. Answers will vary.

LESSON 13

1. Answers will vary.

2. Lucienne: son sèche-cheveux; Sylvie: du shampooing et de l'après-shampooing, une brosse, une brosse à dents, du dentifrice et du déodorant; Patrice: un rasoir, une lotion après-rasage, du savon, une brosse à dents, du dentifrice et un peigne.

3. sèche-cheveux, trousse, shampooing, brosse, dentifrice, déodorant, un rasoir, savon, un peigne

4. le paquet des mouchoirs: 2,80€; le sèche-cheveux de voyage: 15,60€ et le sèche-cheveux plus grand: 25,40€; le shampooing: 2,50€, l'après-shampooing: 2,50€; la brosse: 3€; la brosse à dents: 2,80€; le rasoir: 0,80€; la lotion après-rasage: 3,50€; le savon: 1€; la brosse à dents: 2,80€; le dentifrice: 4,20€; le peigne: 1,40€

5. Answers will vary.

6. du; en bille/en spray; du; pour les cheveux fins/normaux; oui/merci; mouchoirs; un paquet/une boîte

7. Je voudrais du déodorant.; À bille.; Du shampooing.; Pour cheveux fins.; Oui et de l'après-shampooing.; Non, avez-vous du dentifrice?; Et des mouchoirs.; Une boîte.; Oui, c'est tout.

LESSON 14

1. un pantalon, un pull, une chemise, une robe, un sweat shirt; noir, rouge, blanc, noir, bleu marine

2. Monsieur #1: un pantalon noir, taille 42; Madame #1: un pull rouge, taille moyenne; Monsieur #2: une chemise blanche, taille 46; Madame #2: une robe noire, taille 38; Monsieur #3: un sweat-shirt grand en bleu marine

3. 1. b, 2. a, 3. b, 4. a, 5. a
   1. C'est chouette., 2. C'est chic., 3. J'aime la couleur., C'est chic. C'est branché.

4. des bas, des gants, une jupe, un chemisier, des chaussettes, une casquette, un chapeau, des chaussures

5. 1. des chaussures noirs, 2. un soutien-gorge blanc, 3. une robe rouge, 4. des chaussettes avec des rayures bleues et blanches, 5. un sweat shirt gris

6. Answers will vary.

7. Answers will vary.

8. Answers will vary.

9. 1. de grandes chaussures noires, 2. un petit soutien-gorge blanc, 3. une jupe rouge et chic, 4. de chouettes chaussettes avec des rayures bleues et blanches, 5. un sweat-shirt gris branché

10. Answers will vary

LESSON 15

1. 1. avec carte de crédit, 2. avec chèques de voyages, 3. en espèces

2. pink silk tie: 19,75€; green and white striped cotton tie: 15€; plaid wool tie, 17,75€; brown leather tie: 18€

3. red silk scarf: 29,75€; wool scarf: 14,50€; leather gloves: 24€; wool gloves: 13,75€; cotton blouse: 29€; silk blouse: 39,75€

4. a. L'écharpe en soie est plus chère que l'écharpe en laine; b. La chemise en coton est moins chère que la chemise en soie; c. Les gants en cuir sont plus chers que les gants en laine; d. La cravate en cuir marron est moins chère que la cravate en soie rose; e. Le pull en laine est plus cher que le pull en coton.

5. Answers will vary.

6. 1. La jupe est trop courte., 2.Le pull est trop long., 3. Le pantalon est trop large., 4. Le jean est trop cher.

7. 1. e; 2. d; 3. b; 4. a; 5. c

8. 1. La chemise en laine est trop chère., 2. Le pantalon en cuir est plus long que le pantalon blanc.,
    3. La veste en soie est moins chère que la veste rose., 4. Le pull en coton n'est pas cher., 5. La cravate écossaise n'est pas chic.

LESSON 16

1. Charlotte: "Ma mère me conduit au collège en voiture.", Laura: "Je prends le car de ramassage.", Manon: "j'y vais en vélo."; Charlotte: quarante-cinq minutes, Laura: quinze minutes, Manon: vingt minutes

2. Charlotte, voiture, 7:00 a.m.; Laura, le car de ramassage, 7:30 a.m.; Manon, vélo, 7:15 a.m.

3. 1. Non, elle ne prend pas le bus. Elle va en voiture. (No, she doesn't take the bus. She goes by car.), 2. Non, elle ne quitte pas la maison à huit heures. Elle quitte la maison à sept heures et demie. (No, she does not leave the house at 8:00 a.m. She leaves the house at 7:30 a.m.), 3. Non, le voyage ne dure pas quarante minutes pour Manon. Le voyage dure 20 minutes. (No, the ride isn't 40 minutes for Manon. The ride is 20 minutes.)

4. car, 20 min; bus, a good half hour; train, 45 min; bike, 10 min; subway, 15 min; walking, 2 min

5. a. (vous) prenez, partez, arrivez; b. (tu) prends, pars, arrives

6. Answers will vary.

7. a. aller à pied/c'est bon pour la santé; b. aller en moto/c'est plus pratique; c. aller en voiture/c'est plus confortable; d. prendre le train/c'est plus rapide; e. prendre le bus/c'est moins cher; f. prendre un taxi/il n'y a pas de problème avec le parking; g. prendre le métro/c'est rapide

8. Answers will vary.

1. l'Arc de Triomphe, la Tour Eiffel, les Halles, Sacré Coeur;, métro, bus, aller à pied

2. le Musée d'Orsay: 12; la Cité des Sciences: 7; le Louvre: 8; les Halles: 1

3. 1. Oui, Oui, 2. Oui, 3. Non.

5. The trip takes a half hour. I go by subway. I leave at 7:15 a.m. and go to the subway station. I take the subway in the direction of Château de Vincennes which comes every 5 minutes. I arrive at 7:45 a.m.

6. 1. J'ai besoin d'un billet pour aller au Louvre., 2. Non, il vous faut un carnet., 3. On va au Musée d'Orsay., 4. Il faut combien de temps pour aller à l'Arc de Triomphe?, 5. C'est bien le bus pour aller aux Halles?

LESSON 18

1. au théâtre, au Louvre; une demi-heure, vingt minutes

2. 1. Il pleut., 2. C'est cher.

3. un taxi, prendre, il pleut, appeler, ce n'est pas loin; à l'aéroport, trente-cinq, une heure, c'est cher

4. Je voudrais un taxi pour aller à l'aéroport., Le vol part à 17h45., Il met combien de temps?, Ça coûte combien?

5. 1. Quelle sorte de voiture voulez-vous ?; 2. Pour combien de personnes ?; 3. Comment vous appelez-vous ?; 4. Vous voulez la voiture pour combien de jours ?; 5. Vous la voulez quand exactement ?;
   6. Vous avez votre permis de conduire avec vous ?; 7. Comment voulez-vous payer ?; 8. Votre adresse?

6. 1. Une grande voiture.; 2. Six personnes.; 3. Sylvie Verlaine.; 4. Trois jours.; 5. De vendredi à lundi.;
   6. Oui, je l'ai ici.; 7. Avec une carte de crédit.; 8. Hôtel du Parc, rue St-Denis.

7. Answers will vary.

8. Sample questions: Que voulez-vous ?, Quelle sorte de voiture ?, Quand voulez-vous partir ?, Où voulez-vous aller ?, Quel est votre nom ?, C'est combien ?, Comment voulez-vous payer ?

TEST 2

1. 1. c; 2. f; 3. d; 4. e; 5. a; 6. b

2. 1. d; 2. a; 3. c; 4. b; 5. e

3. 1. à la; 2. à l'; 3. à la; 4. au; 5. au; 6. à l'

4. 1. c ; 2. e ; 3. a ; 4. d ; 5. b

5. 1. mon; 2. mes; 3. ma; 4. mon; 5. mes; 6. mon

6. 1. blanche; 2. blanches; 3. blanc; 4. blanche; 5. blancs

7. 1. c; 2. a; 3. b; 4. d

8. 1. il; 2. elle; 3. il; 4. elles; 5. ils; 6. il

9. 1. Vous; 2. Tu; 3. Tu; 4. Vous; 5. Tu; 6. Tu

10. 1. f; 2. d; 3. c; 4. b; 5. e; 6. a.

11. 1. Quelle; 2. combien; 3. Quand; 4. Que; 5. Comment; 6. Où

Photo Credits

LESSON 15

(149) ©2010 Fotolia/Suprijono Suharjoto
(152) Nowik.Shutterstock.2010, arbit.Shutterstock.2010
(153) Andresr.Shutterstock.2010

LESSON 16

(159) ©iStockphoto.com/Tomas Bercic
(162) Kurhan.Shutterstock.2010, Kurhan.Shutterstock.2010,
    Kurhan.Shutterstock.2010, ©2010 Fotolia/Yahia LOUKKAL,
    ©2010 Fotolia/A_nik, melkerw.Shutterstock.2010
(167) ©iStockphoto.com/Chris Schmidt

LESSON 17

(169) Edyta Pawlowska.Shutterstock.2010
(170) Valua Vitaly.Shutterstock.2010, jackhollingsworthcom, LLC.Shutterstock.2010
(175) Yuri Arcurs.Shutterstock.2010
(176) Johnathan Larsen.Shutterstock.2010, fdimeo.Shutterstock.2010, Christian
    Musat.Shutterstock.2010, ©2010 Fotolia/Ewa Walicka

LESSON 18

(179) ©2010 Fotolia/lite
(181) ©2010 Fotolia/Brian Jackson
(182) ©2010 Fotolia/olly
(185) Andresr.Shutterstock.2010, melkerw.Shutterstock.2010
(187) Andriianov.Shutterstock.2010

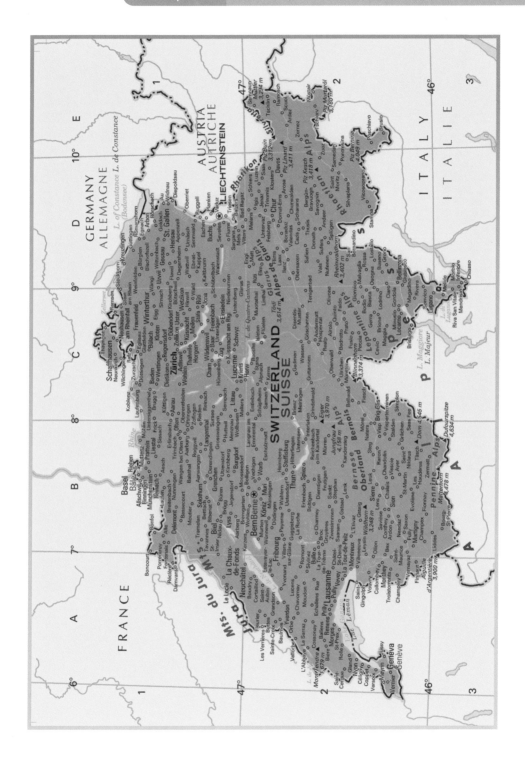

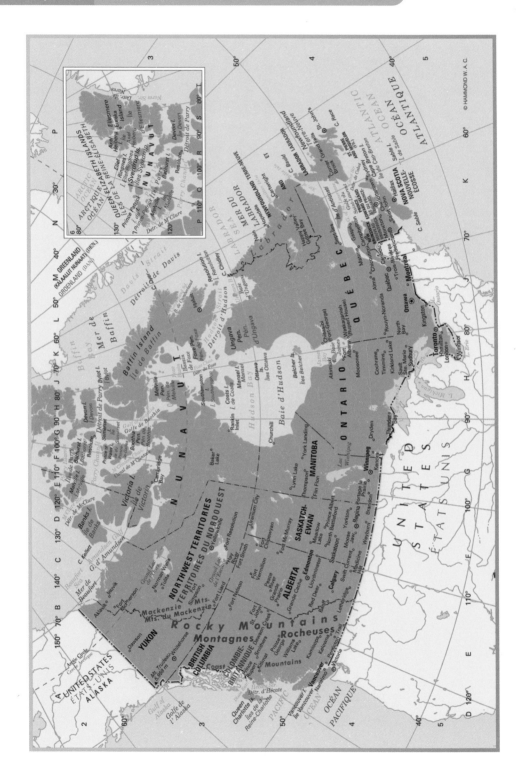

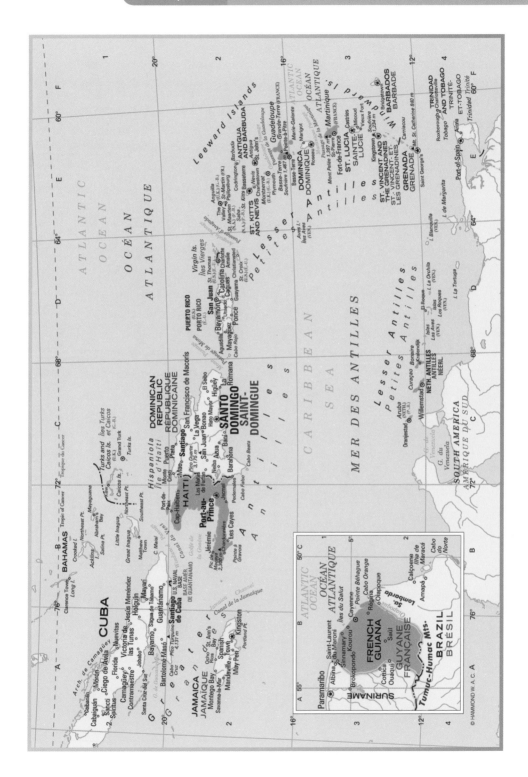

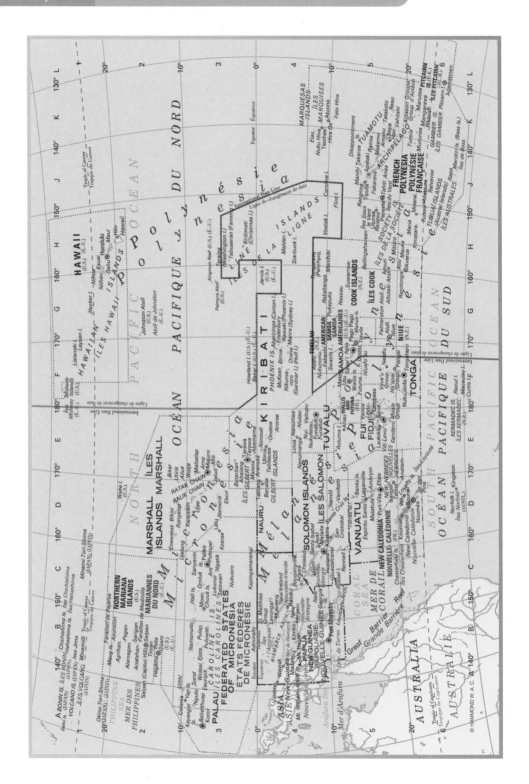

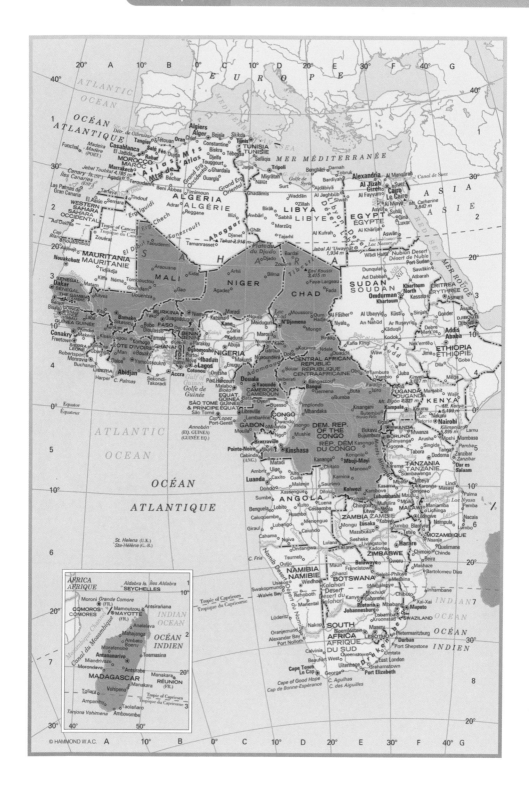